FLYING
PAINT ROLLERS
FROM HEAVEN

Messages of Hope, Humor and Love from Beyond

andy myers, psychic medium

Published by WriteLife
(An imprint of Boutique of Quality Books
Publishing Company)
www.writelife.com

© Cover Photo Designed by:
Kristy Stark Knapp, Knapp Studios

Printed in the United States of America

ISBN 978-1-60808-089-2 (p)
ISBN 978-1-60808-095-3 (e)

First Edition

Dedication

Frances Myers (my late grandma) - It all started with you. Thanks for being the catalyst for my intuitive journey. I miss you and love you so much. Enjoy the sunsets in Heaven.

Acknowledgments

Kenzie Myers (my wife) - Thanks for your unconditional love and loyalty. You are an amazingly beautiful soul, and I love you more than words can describe.

Sue Myers (my mom) - Thanks for your strength, your belief in me, and for being the rock of the family. I couldn't have done this without you. Look how far we've come!

Elizabeth Myers (my sister) - Thank you for your humor, bubbly nature, and constant support. Your light shines brightly and I'm so proud of you for helping others with your intuitive healing.

Terry Oswald (my aunt) - Your generosity never ceases to amaze me. Thanks for your mentoring and for always pushing me to help others. You're a tremendous inspiration!

Zico (my dog) - Thanks for the thousands of hours you've spent with me in readings, helping our clients to relax. You are my angel. Good boy!

Contents

Preface

"Can I ask you one more question?" I hear this phrase uttered from my enthusiastic and uplifted client as the minute hand on the clock ticks past the stopping point of our scheduled session. Glancing at my clock and thinking about my next client who will be arriving shortly, I hesitate. A part of me doesn't want to risk getting off schedule and running behind for the rest of the day.

Looking back at my client's smiling face, I'm compelled by a loving presence to live in the moment and indulge her curiosity. I nestle back into my chair and relax. An unexpected and uncontrolled smile appears on my face as I respond, "Of course you can. What's on your mind?"

This scene happens daily in my office. Everyone always has "one more question." There is a truth seeker within all of us. A child-like curiosity. An unquenchable thirst for knowledge and answers and information. A little inner-inquirer who asks why the sky is blue and how fish breathe underwater and how is it that Christmas lights get so frustratingly tangled from one December to the next. We're curious, all of us. We all have questions. And this is why I decided to write this book in a question-answer format.

This is not the first book written in such a manner, and I'm sure it won't be the last. Over the years, I have been asked tens of thousands of questions by my clients on the subjects of metaphysics, psychic abilities, spirituality, and paranormal phenomena. These questions have ranged from the bizarre and funny to thought-provoking and controversial. My junior high teacher once told me that there is no such thing as a stupid question. We tried to prove him wrong (believe me). But he assured us that any question is valid, as long as it's in the pursuit of knowledge.

I've taken some of the most common and most interesting questions I've received over the years and addressed them in the following pages. Some answers are short, and some are lengthy. I have answered the questions thoroughly and honestly, using my highest level of intuition. I am not the final and all-knowing authority on any matter of life. I believe my well-honed intuition qualifies me to address questions on subjects as important as life, love, God, spirituality, and paranormal phenomena. Let me explain.

On a daily basis, my intuition allows me access to specific and accurate information about my clients. They validate this information during their sessions. I believe it's realistic to assume if my intuition works on a small scale with my clients, then my intuition is accurate and precise when addressing larger issues and questions, such as the ones in this book. Using intuition is the same as accessing truth. It's a direct path to a source that contains all information. Our "human self" does not always have the answers to life's questions, but our intuition resides in the "higher self," and our higher self *does* have the ability to answer life's most baffling questions. Simply put, this book was written by my higher self.

I have categorized the questions into chapters to address one subject at a time and not zig-zag all over the metaphysical map. We'll eventually get from point A to point B on this trip we're about to take together. Let's agree to focus on the journey, not the destination. It's going to be a winding road, with an occasional angel around the bend, a ghost just over the hill, and a few inspirational pit stops along the way.

Sir Arthur Stanley Eddington was a British astrophysicist who did some amazing work studying the luminosity of stars in the early twentieth century. He was a philosopher and a scientist, which in my book qualifies him as "one cool cat." He said, "The universe is not only stranger than we imagine, it's stranger than we *can* imagine." After absorbing the content in this book from cover to cover, I'm confident you'll agree with him.

On this adventure, I'll share true stories with you about life, love, God, and intuition. I'll talk about my crazy cat and a guardian angel named Lefty. There's a tale about a gondola in Venice, Italy, that lends proof to the concept of reincarnation. Another story involves a souvenir from the circus that changed my perspective on life. I'll share with you a whopper of a love story, a true account of a husband

and wife whose connection goes beyond this lifetime. I'll even tell you about the time I glimpsed Heaven through my bedroom ceiling.

I hope this book will inspire you and fill you with wonder. My wish is that it will ignite your curiosity and answer your burning questions related to metaphysics and psychic phenomena. This book may give you goose bumps, evoke laughter, and even bring tears to your eyes. This is *not* another "new age" book. This is a canvas. I've painted it with as much humor as inspiration. My experiences are my paintbrush, and my values are the easel on which this canvas rests.

At certain spots in this book, I will illustrate a point by drawing on experiences from my clients and the psychic readings I've given them. Their names have been changed to maintain confidentiality. I promise the stories you'll read in this book are real and have not been embellished in any way. These are first-hand experiences that I've witnessed. The accounts you'll read just might convince you that reality is truly stranger than fiction. I didn't use a ghost writer to complete this book. I wrote it myself with my own fingertips. The irony of a psychic medium using a *ghost* writer makes me laugh. Think about it.

I invite you to step beyond the threshold with me. I ask you to come with me on a journey into the unknown. Pack lightly, and follow closely behind, my friend. If you're willing to have a sense of adventure and keep an open mind, the information in this book has the potential to change your perspective on many aspects of life.

Introduction

My grandmother once threw a paint roller at me from Heaven. True story. Allow me to explain.

After Grandma Myers passed away, I bought her house and lived there, enjoying all the smells, fond memories, and nostalgia that went along with her charming little home. She was my best friend when she was alive. Living in her house allowed me to feel her loving presence nearly every single day, as she visited me in spirit.

One day, as I painted the kitchen walls, I asked out loud, "Well, Grandma, how do you like the new paint color?" There was no immediate answer. A few minutes later, I went downstairs to wash out the paintbrushes and clean the metal paint roller. The paint roller rested at the bottom of a deep utility sink. I crossed the room to get some old towels from a cabinet, and as I turned back around, I saw the paint roller in mid-air, headed my way. It crashed to the floor and skidded to a stop at my feet. Last time I checked, paint rollers cannot hop out of a two-foot deep wash basin and fly through the air by themselves. I was left with only two possible explanations. Either I had officially lost my mind and was hallucinating, or my grandma took time out of her busy schedule in Heaven to give me a sign that she liked the kitchen's new paint color. This astonishing event really happened, and it's something I will never forget. Experiences like this continue to leave me slack-jawed in amazement, but let's backtrack and start at the beginning of my psychic journey.

When I was eight-years-old, my brother and I saw a kitchen cabinet slowly and eerily swing wide open all by itself. Nobody else was home. We had an unobstructed view of the hair-raising incident. There were no pets in the house that could have been the culprits, and there was no breeze or gust of wind present at the time. No canned goods or food items had fallen off of the shelf or knocked the cabinet door open. There was no explanation. We both looked at each other, wide-eyed in amazement. I'm sure had it not been for our pride, we would have each bolted from the room so quickly it would have lit our socks on fire. This was one of my earliest encounters with the world of the paranormal. It wouldn't be my last.

I'll never know what invisible force opened that kitchen cabinet. In hindsight, I believe the experience was symbolic. It was a gesture from the universe. A sign from above. A precursor to a life filled with mystery, intuition, wonder, and messages from beyond. I believe the open kitchen cabinet symbolized the threshold into a strange new world. An invitation. I eventually accepted this offer.

Oh my goodness! How rude of me. I almost forgot to introduce myself. My name is Andy Myers. I'm the middle of three children with an older brother and a younger sister. Much like me, my sister Elizabeth, was hit by the intuitive branch of the family tree. My mom Sue raised the three of us by herself after our dad died when I was sixteen-years-old. She did a darn fine job of it too, might I add. Throughout my childhood and teen years, I stayed extremely busy playing soccer, and it grew into a passion for me. My elementary school teachers sent me home with plenty of disciplinary warnings and notes. In my defense, free-spirited, creative, intuitive little kids don't always jive with a strict Catholic school environment.

Those who knew me as a child reported I was always a sensitive, kind, and emotional little guy who wore my heart on my sleeve. Being physically and emotionally more sensitive than those around me, I perceived the world differently. I often knew what was about to happen before it happened. However, I wouldn't understand my *sixth* sense until my early twenties. Throughout high school and into college, I constantly had dreams that would later come true. This intrigued me and frustrated me, because I was never able to determine which dreams would later come true and which ones would not.

While making my way through college, I worked at nearly every kind of human services job and mental health facility you can imagine. In hindsight, I realize that while I was working in the social work field, I was honing my intuition without realizing it. My clients and I both benefited when I was intuitively able to know what was wrong with them. Instinctively knowing what help they required and being able to predict their next move was a valuable asset to have.

I earned a Bachelor's Degree in Social Work from the University of Nebraska at Omaha. After using my degree for a few years in the human services field, I began to actively use my intuitive skills by giving psychic readings to willing guinea pigs (usually my sister's friends). The accuracy and specificity of my readings grew, and with time, so did confidence in my gift. Word began to spread like a California wildfire in July, and before I knew it, most of my free time was occupied by these "practice readings."

The universe plopped opportunities into my lap at all the right junctures, leading me to believe I could make a living with my intuition. Opportunity not only came knocking at my door, but it rang my doorbell, too, and let itself into my life with the spare house key! Soon, I was invited onto Omaha's most popular radio station to take questions from callers and provide psychic information.

With an ever-growing list of clients and a calendar full of appointments, I took my mentor's advice and decided to make a go of "the psychic thing" full time on the first day of 2010. I haven't looked in my rear view mirror since. Each year, I say to the world that all I want for Christmas is a never-ending supply of clients to help and people to inspire. So far, I've been given that gift. I say a prayer of gratitude each day for the privilege of doing what I love for a living. Helping others with my intuition is not only my profession, but it's my passion and life purpose.

To date, I've given around 3,700 *documented* psychic

readings to individuals all over the country, and countless undocumented readings via radio and large gallery events. To say I stay busy is an understatement. In addition to my daily psychic readings, I teach classes on various subjects related to intuition, metaphysics, and spirituality. I've given lectures and gallery readings in cities around the country and have been a regular keynote speaker at the annual Omaha Health Expo.

Someone once asked me, "So, what kind of psychic are you?" I briefly paused to ponder this before responding, "The good kind." Although caught off guard by the question, I knew what the person meant. It's a valid question. What kind of psychic am I? Unlike Madam Esmeralda hunched over her crystal ball behind the beaded curtain in a dark and ominous basement, I am dedicated to proving psychics do not have to be flamboyant, phony, or shrouded in mystery. Intuition is natural and can be as down to earth as grandma's apple pie.

I do not use tarot cards in my sessions. Never have. Crystal balls are not welcome in my office either. Unless we're going to hang it from the ceiling, throw on some bell-bottoms, and boogie down to some groovy music, I wouldn't know what to do with a crystal ball. Props don't have anything to do with my intuition. A psychic reading with me is not much different than having a conversation with an old friend.

When giving an intuitive reading, I use a combination of senses. I can hear messages from my client's guardian angels. I can identify the numerous guardian angels by name and explain how they are active in my client's life on a daily basis. I rely heavily on these spirit guides to divulge facts about my client's past, present, and future.

In our sessions, I receive messages and information from my client's loved ones who are in Heaven. This means I'm considered a psychic medium. When the departed in Heaven come through with specific information that can be instantly validated, I'm often as surprised as my client. The process never gets old and never ceases to amaze. I'm just the middle man, tuning my psychic antennae in the general direction of Heaven and relaying to my client the signal I receive.

"Hearing" these messages from guardian angels or loved ones in Heaven has a lot more to do with my heart than it does my ears. I perceive these messages more as an internal whisper, not an external, audible noise. I also *feel* things during a reading that you could label as hunches, gut feelings, or premonitions. While reading clients, I can see images in my mind's eye that relate to their lives, families, careers, futures, health, and past lifetimes. I even see practical images, like my client's downspout needs to be reattached in order to prevent water damage to his basement.

In a psychic reading, I can connect with my client on such a deep and personal level that I will *literally* feel what she is going through, whether it's headaches, depression, knee pain, anxiety, muscle cramps, or vision problems. Temporarily taking on her aches, pains, and emotional stressors gets me one step closer to knowing how to help her. Briefly being in my clients' shoes and literally feeling what she's going through makes me an "empath." Being an empath is a form of intuition that aides me while giving psychic readings.

After a day of giving readings, I'm often reaching for the bottle of Tylenol, because taking on pain from my clients takes a real toll on my body. But I wouldn't change it for the world. Regardless of which intuitive sense I'm using in a reading, it's all enveloped in a blanket of life coaching, which is something I incorporate into each and every reading. It essentially means that I'm offering real, practical, and beneficial guidance. I offer advice and direction that is delivered with the highest degree of empathy and compassion. It's the social worker in me that inevitably comes out during readings. I love my job. I love each and every one of the thousands of people I've met over the years. They've helped me to fulfill my life's work of inspiring and guiding others using my intuition.

Popeye the Sailor always said, "I am what I am and that's all that I am." So who am I? I'm the son of an amazing and generous mother. I'm a brother of two wonderful siblings. I'm a good soccer player with a questionable back and strong legs. I'm an amateur artist. I'm a husband to a marvelous and wonderful wife named Kenzie. I'm a homeowner. I'm a well-traveled individual who looks for beauty in every place and in every person. I'm a psychic, a medium, and a life coach. I'm enthusiastic about life, and I'm a nature-lover. I'm creative. I'm not perfect, and I'm okay with that. I am a work in progress. I am happy. I am grateful. I am *me*.

Well, since we've now been properly introduced, I guess we should get into the meat and potatoes of this book and begin to address the questions at hand. A wise, old philosopher once said that a journey of a thousand miles begins with a single step. We are about to take our first step together on this twisting and turning paranormal journey. I'd like to think of us as travel partners on this trip. Like any adventure, sharing stories with one another is a great way to pass the time. Have I ever told you about my pet walrus?

Chapter 1: Animals

Are animals more sensitive than humans?

My cat is a galloping walrus. Seriously. He has a small head, a bulky, awkward body, and he gallops through the house like a horse that has one leg shorter than the others. Plus, he likes to bathe in the sun for hours on end and has really long, tusk-like teeth. Like I said, he's a galloping walrus if I've ever seen one. I don't tell him this though, because he is *sensitive* and might be offended by my observation of his odd-shaped body and growing waist-line.

I know this is referring to *emotional* sensitivity, and the question has to do with *intuitive* sensitivity, but like a proud parent, I like to take any opportunity possible to talk about my children. Let me tell you a secret: I find it hard to trust a person who doesn't like animals. I can't help but raise a skeptical eyebrow to the person who insists that four-legged critters should remain outside. No, thanks. Not me. They belong inside and on my lap. Even if they resemble a walrus and have a big gut, it's just more of them for me to love. To answer the question, yes, our animals are sensitive, sometimes in an emotional way and oftentimes in a psychic way as well.

How do I know this? Many reasons. First of all, animals are very good at living in the moment. This has everything to do with their intuition, ability to perceive spirits, and intuitive instincts when something is wrong. When we are not preoccupied with guilt and baggage from the past, we are more focused on the "now." Psychic abilities exist in the "now." Our pets don't have anxiety and stress about what the future may or may not bring, which frees up space in the mind for the subconscious to come through.

The subconscious stores all the good stuff: enlightenment, peace of mind, and of course, intuition. We could learn a lot from our furry little four-legged friends about living in the moment. The more you live in the moment, the more you'll be able to access your psychic senses.

The second reason I believe animals are very psychic is because they are pure and innocent. Most of the time. Sometimes. Okay, maybe Fido dug a hole under the backyard fence, escaped, and proceeded to invade old Mrs. Shirley's tomato garden up the street. But he felt very sorry afterward, and if you remember right, he licked your face upon returning home, as if to say "I'm sorry." For all intents and purposes though (tomato garden invasions aside), they are innocent and pure. Animals are much, MUCH better at unconditional love than human beings.

Third, animals instinctively use more senses and *better* senses than we two-legged creatures. Humans have roughly five million scent receptors in our noses, while some species of dogs have as many as 300 million scent receptors. To say that they perceive the world differently than we do would be an understatement. They pick up on subtle vibrations and shifts in energy. Their hearing is impeccable, too (even if they pretend they can't hear you when you tell them to stop sniffing the crotch of your guest). So with all their keen smelling, hearing, sensing, feeling, and seeing, they are bound to be more likely to detect things that we don't, including ghosts and spirits.

They will perceive things too subtle for us to detect. I'm talking mostly about dogs here, because most people can relate to having dogs of their own or at least know of someone who has one. However, cats can be just as intuitive as well, albeit much more neurotic.

Did you hear the story of the psychic cat who lived in a nursing home and could regularly predict the upcoming deaths of its residents? True story. It became national news in 2007. Oscar the cat, lived in the Steer House Nursing and Rehabilitation Center in Providence, Rhode Island. The little fur ball only lived at the facility for two years, but accurately predicted the death of 25 residents at the nursing home by inexplicably becoming attached to a person and refusing to leave their side for weeks leading up to their demise.

Then there was Paul, the Psychic Octopus, who made international news during the summer of 2010 by accurately predicting the results of the German National Soccer Team matches during its run at the World Cup. Paul's owners would place food inside of two different boxes which were in Paul's tank. The boxes were marked with the national flags of Germany and whichever team they happened to be playing next. Seven times in a row, Paul chose to invade the food box of the winning team and in doing so became an international cephalopod celebrity.

Okay, maybe this example is a stretch. Probably just a media marketing ploy. Still, noteworthy and interesting though, if you ask me. They retired Paul from his psychic duties at the end of 2010. I can picture him now, somewhere in Florida, enjoying strawberry daiquiris, listening to Jimmy Buffett, enjoying his senior-citizen discount, and retired from active psychic duty.

Has your dog ever sat straight up out of a dead sleep, stared at the doorway, and growled as if to protect you from some unseen intruder? So has my dog. His name is Zico (pronounced "Zee-Ko"). He's a local celebrity in his own right, and I swear that some of my clients come back to see me time and time again simply to interact with Zico.

Why do our dogs scare us by acting as though they can see an invisible force in our living space? Good question. If your dog suddenly seems startled and barks, growls, or has hair standing on end while protecting you from some unforeseen entity in your house, we have to concede the possibility that they are seeing something that we're not. They could be seeing a ghost, an angel, or a visiting relative from Heaven. Our pets could actually be seeing different visitors at different times.

Let me make something very clear. Something that will provide you with peace of mind. Just because your canine is ferociously growling at an invisible "something" in the room doesn't mean that the dog perceives something bad or threatening. Anything in the room that is *unexpected* or catches your four-legged friend *off guard* will be enough to startle him and throw him into instinctual, protective mode. Due to the different laws of physics governing ghosts, spirits, and angels, they do indeed come and go unexpectedly and suddenly.

So, next time you're thinking that Brutus has sensed the Grim Reaper in the room, just relax. It's possible he is sensing something as pure as an angel from God. In that case, you may really want to keep him from sniffing the crotch of your angelic houseguest. I'm not sure what the protocol for that is, but it would probably make for an awkward situation.

Do our pets go to Heaven?

I always say that if our animals can't go to Heaven, I'm not going either. But the good news is our beloved critters DO make it to Heaven. Your dogs and cats. Your pet parakeet. Your favorite fish, and your terribly terrific tarantula. If you loved them dearly when they were alive, then rest assured they'll be waiting for you in Heaven. And until you arrive there yourself, one of your animal-loving family members in Heaven will keep your pets company. But your loved ones in Heaven may keep the tarantula in its terrarium until you arrive. I don't blame them for that.

I believe that God is a loving and fair Creator. He would not deprive us of the opportunity to be reunited with our loving animal companions. Animals do have souls. Their spirit and their energy is as real and alive as our own. Therefore, they survive the death process. Once "over there," your dog will once again bounce around with the energy and enthusiasm of a puppy. Whether or not he chews a hole in your favorite pair of slippers like he did when he was a puppy, now that's a whole other question. Rest assured that when you cross over and reconnect with your animals in Heaven, they will be absent of any and all health problems they experienced while here on Earth. Truly at the peak of their existence, happier, healthier, and more loyal than ever.

And it's only fair that they're allowed entrance into Heaven. I know plenty of people who feel more connected to animals than they do to humans. These people will be more excited to reunite with their dogs than they will with their grouchy aunt, Rhonda. Animals absolutely deserve to go to Heaven!

We can learn a lot from animals. And we'll have plenty of time to do so when we get the privilege of spending an unlimited amount of time with them on the Other Side. If your cat or ferret or rabbit or dog is sitting with you right now, acting as your reading companion, please squeeze them extra tightly and give them a scratch behind the ears from their Uncle Andy. But when the time comes to let them go, please have an unwavering faith that it's just a temporary goodbye. A "see you later." And when you're someday reconnected with them in Heaven, you'll pick up right where you left off.

Do ghost animals exist?

Ghost animals are very rare, and there is a good reason for this. Like we talked about earlier, animals are living in the moment and are intellectually very simple compared to humans. They do not have the guilt, anxiety, dogma, religious fears, or hesitancies about the unknown that we do. Therefore, the instant their heart stops beating, they are extremely likely to cross through the light and run towards the warm feeling of love without hesitation.

Humans, on the other hand, have been raised with the idea that they could go to a bad place called Hell upon crossing over, if they didn't have their spiritual ducks in a row at the time of their death. This can cause a person to hesitate during the "crossing over" phase and get stuck in the in-between as a ghost. They'll eventually come to their senses and cross over into Heaven. Our loyal pets do not have this complicated thought process at the time of their deaths, and this is why they typically run, bounce, and leap through to the Other Side instantly.

We humans also have lots of baggage from the past and unfinished business, which is another reason that ghosts will typically hang around instead of crossing over. Animals usually do not have unfinished business (unless your dog never got around to peeing on every single bush along his favorite walking path before he died). Our animals can and do cross over into Heaven effortlessly.

Can our loved ones in Heaven give us a sign, message, or validation through animals?

When I was young, I believed in barking spiders for a brief period of time. Why? Because my dad told me they existed. Yep. He blamed barking spiders regularly for unexpected and unexplained noises coming from underneath him. I now know that flatulence can cause a person to lie and place the blame on mythical creatures. I have learned a few other things over the years, including the fact that our loved ones in Heaven do send us *real* animals as a little "hello" or "I love you" from the Other Side.

Why send us animals? Why don't our loved ones just appear to us in our time of need while we're praying? Because it's a heck of a lot easier (energetically) for them to give us signs and messages using objects that already exist in our world and natural surroundings. It's easier for them to make a butterfly land on your shoulder than it is for them to materialize out of thin air and give you a hug.

If your life depended on it, I bet you could run two miles non-stop, even if you haven't exercised in years. Unless you absolutely *had* to do this, I bet you wouldn't attempt to, since it would leave you dangerously fatigued and probably sick. Physically, it's possible to run two miles when you're out of shape, but it would be ill-advised. For this very same reason, our loved ones in Heaven tend to rely on things already existing in our physical environment to give us signs, such as animals. They do this so they don't have to exhaust themselves trying to get our attention.

I was in a reading with a client named Samantha who wanted to connect with her late father. Her father kept giving me images of binoculars and birds. These images kept popping in and out of my head until I asked Samantha if this made any sense to her. "Now that I think about this, it makes perfect sense," she reported. She then explained to me that when her dad passed away, she didn't get to keep many of his belongings, but one thing she did manage to hang on to was his trusty pair of binoculars. "He used them constantly," she said. Samantha told me her dad was an avid bird watcher. Sitting in my office and thinking about it for a second, Samantha realized why she was seeing so many colorful and rare birds around her house. Now, she'll know to say hello back to her dad when the yellow and orange finches are fluttering around her backyard.

In another case, I was talking with a grief-stricken, middle-aged lady named Linda who was carrying a heavy heart due to the loss of many family members. Her deceased aunt came through to me very strongly talking about butterfly bushes, planting, and gardening in general. Linda cracked a smile through the tears, and I saw in her eyes that this message registered as true for her.

"Just last night I was gardening, and I planted a bush in the backyard that is supposed to attract butterflies," she said. I smiled as well and explained that, sometimes, our loved ones give us little hints like this as proof that they are with us even during our day-to-day activities, such as gardening. Linda then explained to me, this particular deceased aunt also loved to garden, which is probably why she was interested enough to be there in spirit for the planting of the butterfly bushes. It's safe to say that her aunt is planning on sending truck-loads of butterflies to those bushes as a sign that she's still alive and well on the Other Side.

So how do you know what animals your loved ones are going to send you from the Other Side? Maybe, they'll keep it simple and cause you to see your favorite animal. In other cases, they'll send *their* favorite animals to you with such frequency and in such abundance that you'll see them everywhere you go. Another way to approach it is to be specific with them. If you want your crazy Uncle Tommy to send you deer, then demand to see deer. Just ask him to keep them off the street and away from your car. While you're at it, can you ask him to keep them away from *my* car, too? Thanks.

If you want to know that your dad still thinks about you from time to time even though he died many years ago, challenge him with something a little more rare, and perhaps ask to see an owl. Or an eagle. Or maybe a raccoon. Just tell him to keep those barking spiders to himself.

If our beloved pets go to Heaven, do animals in the wild go to Heaven, as well?

I've been asked that question live on the radio before, and it really made me think. I guess the caller wanted to play the family friendly game of "Stump the Psychic." I believe our pets go to Heaven, because we love them as much as our human companions, and it's only fair. I would find it hard to believe, though, that every single moose or giraffe that has *ever* lived in the wild has now crossed over into Heaven and has eternal life there.

I do believe intuitively that there are just the right number of wild moose and giraffes in Heaven. I guess it's up to God how many individuals of each species there are. Human beings don't have this problem of overpopulating Heaven, because we don't all stay there forever. We recycle. We come back to Earth, time and time again, for more incarnations. We'll talk more about reincarnation later, so please don't be an "eager beaver" and skip ahead to that chapter. And please, don't ask me how many "eager beavers" are in Heaven. I don't know. What I do know is there are no barking spiders on the Other Side. And there are no mosquitos either. Good riddance.

Can people reincarnate as animals?

This question has me torn, and I have mixed feelings about it. *Personally,* I would like to believe we can live a lifetime as a lazy house cat, a majestic horse, or a loyal seeing-eye dog. I want to believe that we can have that experience to keep in our soul for the sake of diversity and variety. *Intuitively*, however, I do not think that human beings can ever incarnate as an animal species here on Earth. Intuitively, I believe that every time you've been here, you've been human. It's important for us all to distinguish our personal wants from our intuitive truth.

Sometimes they are not one in the same.

I wish we could incarnate as animals. I want it to be true. I could get used to the idea of lounging around the house all day, taking naps at my leisure, while my master works a nine to five job and picks up my treats on the way home. Yes, sir. That would be the life. I would be a good boy and learn many tricks and get many treats. So many treats that my body would become ever more walrus-like, but I wouldn't care because my owner would still love me anyway.

If it were possible, what animal would you want to be? Are you as neurotic and eccentric as a snooty house cat? Would you prefer to be a sea-going creature, such as a playful dolphin? How about a high-flying feathered friend, defying gravity, and seeing the whole world glide beneath you? Think about this for a minute, as you go about your daily business: What animal would you be if you had the choice? You can tell a lot about people based on their choice of animal. When I was young, my mom told me that my room looked like a pig sty. Maybe I would choose to be a pig. Oink, oink.

Are pet psychics for real?

If we're asking this question, we may as well ask, "Are regular psychics for real?" Are chiropractors for real? Are intuitive healers, mystics, astrologers, or miracle workers for real? My answer would be, "Some are, some aren't." Human beings are capable of far more than we give ourselves credit for. We have not yet scratched the surface regarding our true potential and the marvelous feats we are capable of achieving, individually and collectively. I believe in the intuitive, spiritual, and healing gifts themselves, but every now and then, you'll come across a phony person falsely claiming to have a gift that he does not possess.

Do you know why I don't call myself a pet psychic? Because I don't have enough experience in that area. I have not thoroughly been tested in the area of communicating with animals, and I have not been validated enough times to believe I have a special gift in that department. Maybe, someday, I will. But I don't yet. All of us should definitely practice within our scope of knowledge and expertise when it comes to our profession.

I do, however, believe that there are special individuals who can and do communicate with animals psychically. I don't fully understand how this works. Then again, there are a lot of phenomena that we believe, yet don't fully understand. I bet you don't fully understand how eyesight works and yet, your eyes are working well enough to allow you to read these words right now. Aren't they?

What about unicorns, elves, fairies, Bigfoot, and the Loch Ness Monster? Do they exist?

We're getting into weird territory here. I like that. My Grandma Myers would have loved to join in on this conversation. As a young child, I remember her reading me stories from the dusty books in her den. Books about mysteries and monsters and myths. Books about creatures, real, imagined, mythical, or unknown. She was a catalyst in jumpstarting my love for the metaphysical and paranormal. She never forced her opinions onto me, but instead, challenged me to form my own thoughts regarding these creatures and the possibility of their existence.

I'm very open to the idea of mysterious creatures being real. There are a few exceptions, however. I do not believe in vampires. I also do not believe in werewolves. I just can't get on board with the idea of human beings suddenly growing excess body hair, fangs, and superhuman strength, while they pillage and terrorize the neighborhood during a full moon. My Uncle Art is a pretty hairy guy, but not even he could be accused of werewolfing around. Sorry to all of you *Twilight* fans out there, but bloodsucking vampires and hairy werewolves are two creatures that will have to stay in our imaginations and in movie theaters.

Regarding the other unknown or unidentified creatures, I subscribe to two different possibilities. Sometimes thought, consciousness, and the collective societal belief in something creates enough energy to manifest the thought into reality. Therefore, it's *possible* that Bigfoot and the Loch Ness Monster *are* real in the sense that they have come into reality just because people believe in them so adamantly. We manifested them into our reality. We created them. We conjured them out of thin air into a physical entity. That's one possibility. Human thought is more powerful than neuroscientists can grasp, therefore, we must entertain this concept.

This may sound crazy until you take into account the other marvelous feats that the human brain has already accomplished. There are documented accounts of Tibetan monks who have become so skilled at meditation they can sit on frigidly cold mountain tops overnight wearing light cloth robes that are soaked in water. Through the power of thought alone, they are able to maintain a completely normal skin temperature, whereas, a normal person would freeze to death in less than an hour. If our brains can do this, why can't our brains accomplish other amazing feats, such as bringing a creature into existence from the world of imagination? Doing so is sometimes referred to as creating *tulpas.*

My second thought on the matter of unknown or mythical creatures has a more scientific spin on it. Cryptozoology is a legitimate science for which some universities offer courses of study. This is the study of unknown, undiscovered, and unexpected creatures. Cryptozoologists spend their free time trudging through jungles, swamps, and desolate mountain ranges, hot on the trail of species they believe to be real.

They are avid researchers who conduct interviews and attempt to debunk false reports in pursuit of the truth. Many of the reports of mythical creatures have a sliver of truth to them, and as crazy as some of the stories may sound, we owe it to ourselves to keep an open mind.

That said, I'm right there with you in thinking that some of the witnesses to these strange creature sightings may have had one too many beers leading up to their encounters. Some documentaries and evening news interviews will decrease credibility by talking with "Billy-Bob" who swears that he and his trusty basset hound "done seen the hairy beast trying to steal his pickup truck, and by the time he and Ol' Buck took another drink of moonshine, the hairy feller disappeared over yonder behind them there trees." To all you cryptozoologists out there, I salute you for weeding out cases like this to get the scoop on the more reliable sightings from credible and honest witnesses.

Have you ever seen anything odd or unexpected? If you have, did you mention it to anyone? If not, I completely understand. We all have a reputation of sanity to uphold. Then again, if everyone is seeing odd creatures, but nobody is talking about them, doesn't that make you think that there *are* things out there that science has simply not been able to validate yet? There are dozens of new creatures identified and discovered each year around the world. Some of them are not small, either!

For example, a new species classified as the "snub-nosed monkey" was found for the first time as recently as 2010 in the country of Myanmar. We're not talking about an itty-bitty bug here that went undetected by scientists. We're talking about a *monkey!* If an animal such as this, larger than a well-fed house cat, can go undiscovered for so long, just imagine what other types of creatures are out there waiting to be found.

In recent years, fisherman and deep sea explorers have proven for the first time that the Kraken (the giant squid) actually does exist and is not a mere legend. Japanese scientists were exploring at depths of 3,000 feet off the coast of Japan and caught video of a giant squid measuring twenty-six feet. The creature took the bait, but eventually freed itself, leaving behind an eighteen-foot long tentacle. Until then, the giant squid was thought to exist only in people's imaginations and science fiction books.

Maybe, these mysterious creatures already exist in the wild and are elusive enough to avoid human detection for the time being. Perhaps, they didn't exist until enough people collectively believed in them and manifested them into reality. Either way, they may be out there. I want to assure you that just because a creature is unknown or still mysterious to us doesn't mean it's scary. It doesn't mean the creature is evil and waiting for the chance to feast on our brains for dinner. They could be gentle giants or as lovable as your family pet. As far as unicorns, maybe they're just misidentified horses wearing pointed birthday party hats. I don't know.

Andy, what is your favorite animal?

My pets, of course. Which specific pet? That's not fair. I can't play favorites. I love my cat, Darwin, the galloping walrus, for his uncanny knack of cuddling with me at just the right time, and for his indifferent attitude towards life itself. I love my dog, Zico, for his amazing loyalty. Did you know that Zico has literally been in thousands of psychic readings with me, providing comfort, encouragement, and support to clients who walk into my office? I also admire his sheer resiliency. Zico shouldn't even be alive right now. Yep, if my dog were a cat with nine lives, he would have blown right through eight of them in the first year I had him.

Zico was six months young when I adopted him from the Humane Society. The first week, I took him to my co-worker's house which was on a few acres of land in the middle of nowhere. While I was there, Zico roamed free and promptly made his way into a bull corral. Yes, a *bull corral*! The bull was only half the problem though, because as the ferocious beast charged scrawny little Zico with the business end of its horns, the horse in the corral kicked Zico right in the ribs and sent his 30-pound body sailing through the air like a Frisbee. His ego was bruised, but no bones were broken.

A year later, Zico rummaged through the bathroom garbage can and decided it was a good time to eat some disposable razor blades. The vet did x-rays and said the outcome would not be good unless they removed the shards from his stomach in an emergency surgery. He recovered and has the tummy scar to prove it. I told him that all he needed to accompany his cool scar were some tattoos, and he would be the bad boy (dog) on the block.

For his next stunt, he played in and drank blue algae water all afternoon at a state park campground before I noticed the signs warning that blue algae can be extremely toxic and kill small animals. Again, he laughed in the face of death and lived to tell the story. Last, but not least, as a puppy, he chewed up and destroyed an entire collection of my soccer DVDs. He almost didn't survive that experience, because I wanted to kill him *myself*. In the end, we are always quick to forgive those we love most. I love my pets and I love all animals. Aside from my daredevil dog and my galloping walrus? I like hawks. They are my favorite animals. Hawks don't eat my DVDs. Or razor blades.

Chapter 2: Spirituality

Is being psychic a God-given gift?

Yes, it is. It's a gift from God. Some of us are born with the ability to paint beautiful pictures. Some of us are born with Herculean strength and athleticism. Others can solve complex mathematical puzzles in their heads. And some individuals are born with a God-given gift to feel energy around themselves and others, and intuitively *know* things using their sixth sense.

I would consider myself a pretty easy going person. I do not have road rage. I go with the flow. I'm not prone to bouts of anger very often, and it really takes quite a bit to push my buttons. However, one thing that really gets me fired up is when people suggest that intuition or any form of psychic abilities is "fraternizing with the devil."

If you stop and think about it for a minute, this doesn't make any rational, logical sense. If intuition is a gift that is being shared with others, for the sake of others, giving them inspiration, encouragement, and a sense of direction in life, wouldn't God *want* us to use our intuition? Aside from that, what good is a talent, skill, or gift if we aren't supposed to use it? It would be such a waste. What if Mozart never decided to touch a piano because people accused him of witchcraft? What if Michelangelo walked away from his paintbrushes because others told him it was somehow unholy? This would have deprived the world of some pretty amazing art.

If intuition is misused for selfish or manipulative reasons, I whole-heartedly believe that God can take it away, just as easily as He gave it to us. Some of the fear-based individuals out there who think psychics are doing Satan's dirty work simply don't understand what it means to be intuitive. Everyone is intuitive. *Everyone.* The term "mother's intuition" does not carry negative connotations. Why? Because it's natural for a mother to be connected to her children in such a strong, spiritual sense that she simply *knows* what is best for the children and instinctively *knows* how to keep her offspring away from harm. I'd like to believe we are ALL connected to one another in this deep spiritual sense, which is why any one person is intuitive enough to help any other person using their God-given psychic senses.

Is God male or female?

Both and neither. In my humble opinion, God is a life force that contains energy which could be labeled as both "masculine" and "feminine." God is in us, and we are in God. We are inseparable. Therefore, if God lacks traits that are nurturing, loving, supporting, emotional, sensitive, and all the other qualities we view as "feminine," then so do we. If God lacks logic, strength, and other qualities we stereotypically view as "masculine," then we lack these traits as well. Furthermore, gender stereotypes are breaking down all the time and there are both masculine *and* feminine traits within all of us.

God does not have a physical body. Therefore, He does not have a penis. She does not have lady parts. In this respect, God would technically and scientifically be neither male nor female. God is a life force; an energy made up of all the best qualities we collectively exhibit as a human species. Throughout this book I'll often refer to God as "He," but please know that I'm not suggesting God is more masculine than feminine. I only do this because it's a heck of a lot easier to type *and* read "He" than "He/She/It."

How do I open myself up spiritually, so I can access my intuition more often?

Before we continue further down this mineshaft of questions, I want to clarify that the words "psychic" and "intuitive" can be used interchangeably. They are one in the same. I hope that helps. Down we go. Keep your arms and legs inside the ride at all times.

First of all, take some pressure off yourself. This question is often asked by people who are anxious and bursting at the seams to tap into their well of intuition but are frustrated at not getting immediate and mind-blowing psychic results. To "open yourself up spiritually" implies there is a blockage of some kind. If you're open and eager enough to ask this question then, you're probably doing better than you think you are, and are not psychically blocked. It's a good question to ponder though, because it's a fact that being more *spiritually* centered will help you be more *intuitively* centered.

If you are more spiritual, you will be more psychic. The question then comes full circle: "How do I become more spiritual?" By going to church? Meditating more? Volunteering or donating to charity? Getting out and being one with nature every day? My answer is "Yes, yes, yes, and yes." My personal standard of spiritual centeredness may be different than your spiritual standard. Any and all of those things may work for you. Some of them may work more efficiently than others. It depends on who you are and what tickles your fancy. When it comes down to it, we're merely talking about trial and error. Find a way to get your spiritual jollies and stick with it for a while. If one particular method doesn't work for you, change your routine. Our good friend, Albert Einstein, was once quoted as saying, "Insanity is doing the same thing over and over again and expecting different results."

If you take a walk in the park every day for a week and don't feel one ounce more enlightened or intuitive, then try something else. If you've been going to the same church for two years, and it's not quite doing it for you, then try a different church. Or try meditation. Or a hot bath. Or a spiritual discussion group. Mix it up, for God's sake (and your own).

I'll let you in on a little secret of life that I've accidentally stumbled across while jumping from one spiritual lily pad to another: God, happiness, and peace of mind cannot be found externally. They must be found internally. If you go on some wild goose chase looking for the spiritual key to happiness, you're not going to find it. It's only when we stand still enough to look inwardly that we will find a sliver of God and a slice of joy. Keep this in mind as you try to open yourself up and tap into your psychic senses.

When you're sitting on the edge of a swimming pool, looking down, and kicking your feet, you can't see the bottom of the pool because of all the commotion and bubbles. It's only when you sit still and stop kicking that you can see the bottom of the pool clearly. Life is like this. Stop kicking. Stop struggling. Stop causing so much commotion, and just relax. When you do, everything becomes clearer.

Does God get mad at us for taking his name in vain or cursing?

Heck no, He doesn't. God does not judge people for swearing. Personally, I use profanity *very* rarely. I'm just not good at it. It doesn't come naturally to me. Plus, it leaves me with a bad taste in my mouth. Like drinking orange juice right after I've brushed my teeth. Yuck. Cursing just doesn't make me feel relaxed. It raises my blood pressure.

Yet, there are some people who curse in such creative and innovative ways that it almost sounds like they're reciting poetic profanity. God does not look down on these people any more than He would look down on a toddler for throwing a temper tantrum or the artist who writes graffiti all over the side of a building. These are all forms of self-expression. Sure, some forms of expression are healthy and some are detrimental.

God knows all of life is a learning process. God knows each of us is wonderfully and eccentrically different, therefore, we all need to express ourselves uniquely. God knows that no form of self-expression is necessarily better or worse than another because self-expression, even through language, is a huge part of why we're here making our way through life: to lose ourselves, find ourselves, create ourselves, *re-create* ourselves, and to figure out who we are and what we stand for. This is a monumental piece to the puzzle of life. Language (all parts of it) can be a part of this journey.

Those who are tossing around "F-bombs" like candy at a parade may be doing it out of anger, to impress their buddies, or simply as filler in the story they are telling. I once heard my brother drop three "F-bombs" in one short sentence that contained no more than ten words. To this day, I'm not quite sure how he pulled off such a tongue twisting feat of the English language, but, by God, he did it. Part of me was amazed and impressed. Part of me was appalled. But I didn't judge him, because I knew God wasn't judging him for this either.

What about people who have the audacity to take our great Creator's name in vain? For all of you familiar with the Bible, this is the Third Commandment, right? "Thou shall not take the Lord thou God's name in vain." I know that right now you have a nagging voice in the back corners of your brain that has been fueled by a lifetime of religious teachings. It's saying that taking the Lord's name in vain must be on God's "no-no" list if it's important enough to be engraved on those slabs of stone Moses hauled down from the mountain all those years ago. Please try to remain open-minded here, as I tell you it doesn't offend God in the slightest or hurt his feelings when "the goddamn car" cuts you off and nearly runs you off the road during rush hour.

Don't get me wrong here. I'm not advocating that it's now open season to spew a foul-mouthed rant to the high Heavens and blame God for all our Earthly problems. I'm just stating that because God is above pettiness and practices forgiveness on a scale we cannot fully comprehend. He is not going to hold a grudge against us for cursing His name.

Again, we must keep in mind that God knows we are generally doing the best we can with the cards we've been dealt in life. He knows we slip up. He even expects it. We're a work in progress, aren't we? God knows we're trying to find ways to express ourselves and the strong emotions we feel on our journey through life.

On the north side of Omaha, near where I used to live, there is a billboard on the side of a busy street which always bothers me as I drive by. It's a big old behemoth of a sign. In black and white, it reads, "Keep taking my name in vain, and I'll make rush hour even longer. –God." My problem with this is that it suggests God is vengeful. It implies that if we do something mean to God, then God will get us back by doing something mean to us. Retaliation like this is not a good quality, and personally, it's not a quality I'd expect from an all-loving, all-forgiving God.

Logically, why would we be okay with a God who reciprocates with unkind acts if we don't even want our *toddlers* reciprocating with unkind acts? If someone hits your kid, you don't tell your kid to punch back. Hate breeds more hate. This is why the billboard doesn't make logical sense to me. And it's part of the reason I believe God cuts us a break for using his name in vain, gosh darn it.

Is there a certain prayer or meditation that works better than others?

Somebody once told me that prayer is talking to God, and meditation is listening to God. That stuck with me, and I think it's an interesting way to view things. In general, I think most of us are a lot better at asking questions than we are at listening for answers.

First of all, let's talk about prayer. There are as many prayers as there are drops of water in the ocean. The more traditional image that comes to mind involves somebody in church, head bowed in respect, hands folded, lips silently mouthing a prayer with utmost reverence and respect. Others who subscribe to a more personal, spiritual approach take a stroll through the woods and thank God for the smell of the flowers, the warmth of the sun, and the beauty of the sky. Other people half-way around the world may be lying flat on their backs next to a bonfire, counting the stars, and making wishes on each of them. They may not even know they're praying, but they are.

I happen to do some of my best praying in the bathroom. Hey, don't judge me! God does some of His best listening while I'm in there, so it works out just fine, thank you very much. We have good conversations in the bathroom, God and I. The only problem is that, sometimes, while praying, I get distracted by my own wandering mind. I'm sure that God is patient and understands that I sometimes lose my train of thought. Does this ever happen to you? I bet it does. God knows we sometimes have the attention span of a hamster under the influence of Red Bull. He doesn't mind that our thoughts get sidetracked while chatting with Him. If you've ever fallen asleep while praying, rest assured you're not alone. Happens to me all the time. I don't think it counts as a "failed" prayer though. Lord knows we're tired and need our beauty sleep.

There's no right or wrong way to do it. Prayer is prayer, and God is always listening. Prayers of gratitude are some of my favorites, but no particular prayer is more beneficial or effective than another. They all have different purposes, and they all have their places. If I could make one small suggestion, please remember that gratitude attracts more wealth, health, happiness, and whatever else you're looking for in life. We must first be grateful, and then it's absolutely within reason to ask for more of anything.

If you feel guilty for praying for yourself, *don't*! If you were raised with the belief that it's selfish to pray for yourself, I challenge you to question the logic of this. It's not self-centered to pray for yourself, especially if you're praying for the strength to be the best person you can be. And what if you're praying for the wisdom to be of assistance to others? I'm sure God doesn't have a problem with that. After all, He *wants* us to help one another. In this crazy journey of life, we're all in this together, and sometimes, we have to carry the wounded so they don't get left behind. It's hard work. Ask God to give you the strength to keep going.

Can our loved ones in Heaven see what we're doing *all* the time?

I think a better question is, "Would they even *want* to?" We do some pretty weird things. Come on. You have to admit it. I'll admit that I demonstrate some fairly odd behaviors when nobody is looking. Have you ever noticed that you have a hole in your sock but wear it anyway, figuring nobody will see it because you're not taking your shoes off until you're back in the comfort of your own home? Have you ever covered your mouth while sneezing and accidentally soaked your hand with your own saliva, but there wasn't a tissue handy so you had to coyly wipe it on your pants and just get on with the day? You haven't? Okay then, in that case, neither have I.

These are the things our spirit guides and loved ones *can* see from Heaven, if they choose to be with us at that particular moment. The good news is they're not judging. And they have probably done something even stranger, once upon a time.

Going from the gross moments to the intimate moments, rest assured when things start heating up in the bedroom, grandpa, mom, your spirit guides, and anyone else looking over you in spirit takes the cue to exit. Plus, they've been in the human condition before, so they know what's going on and don't want to overstep their boundaries. Just imagine your spirit helpers winking at you and saying, "Go get 'em tiger. I'll be here later if you need me." Again, there is no judging on their part. Ever.

In many of my psychic readings, clients expect me to relay meaningful messages from their loved ones in Heaven. I gladly oblige, but sometimes, I'm as amazed as they are by what comes through. Oftentimes, their loved ones give me little hints they are around my client much of the time, keeping them company on a daily basis and taking an active interest in what they're doing.

Some sweet ladies who were at one of my speaking events raised their hands, and when I called on them, they asked if I could tell them anything about someone whom they had just lost. The information came through very rapidly. It was their mom. I sensed she died recently, and she wanted me to mention "car air fresheners."

As soon as I relayed the message from their deceased mom, the sisters not only confirmed that she died recently, but also laughed hysterically, and said they knew why she told me to bring up car air fresheners. Apparently, earlier in the week they had just begun using their mom's car for the first time since her death, and they lovingly joked at how wonderfully horrible the air freshener smelled. It was too potent! It was an assault on their nostrils, and they got a big kick out of how stinky mom's car was. Although this wasn't the most moving or emotionally-charged message in the world, it made their night. Why? Because it helped prove their mom can see what they're doing on a daily basis and is still with them to share in their laughs, even if her car was the butt of the joke.

Another example comes from a phone reading I did with a girl named Cassie, on live radio in Kansas City. Her deceased grandfather came through saying, "The bookcase needs to be repaired." After I told her this, Cassie told me her grandfather was into yard sales, garage sales, and flea markets, always looking for a good bargain. She also said she and her family just conducted a garage sale of their own and had a hard time getting rid of grandpa's old bookcase, which was in need of some repair. Her grandfather may not be with Cassie every second of the day, but you can bet your bottom dollar he was present at the family yard sale.

Meeting with a different client named Tiffany who also lost her father, we received more confirmation that our loved ones absolutely DO see what we're doing day in and day out. Her deceased father wanted me to bring up a mishap that Tiffany recently had with milk. Her dad said this to me in a matter-of-fact way, and I could feel him winking and smiling at me, as if his daughter would know what this message was all about. I eagerly relayed this message to Tiffany, and I was interested to hear her reaction.

She slapped her knee and started cracking up, while telling me about a breakfast fiasco she had a few hours prior to our reading. She said that before coming to my office, she accidentally used twice the amount of milk that was called for in the pancake recipe. It validated for Tiffany that although her dad was in Heaven, he was not too busy to stop by in spirit, and have breakfast with her that very morning.

Some dads are there to have breakfast with us, and some dads are there to help us with home improvement projects. While doing a medium session with Anna, her deceased father came through and wanted me to bring up "the water pressure getting fixed." Anna filled me in on the fact that two days prior to our reading, she and her husband *finally* got the water pressure in their house adjusted. I can just imagine Anna's dad in spirit form, standing over the shoulder of the plumber, making sure he was doing everything correctly and not cutting corners. You know how some dads are.

Another example comes from a reading I gave live on Q98.5 FM radio in Omaha. The holidays were quickly approaching, and a nice guy named William called into the station, asking me if his deceased mom ever comes around him this time of year. He missed her so much it hurt. I could hear William's mom. She wanted me to tell him, "When you get a haircut, don't let them change it too much. You're handsome just how you are, and I love your hair." William's response was one of disbelief. He explained to everyone listening that he was calling from his car, and was sitting in the parking lot of the salon, waiting for them to open so he could get a haircut. It was safe to say, beyond a shadow of a doubt, that William's mom visits him in spirit much of the time, especially around the holidays.

Our loved ones in Heaven see our milk mishaps, garage sales, plumbing projects, and haircuts. They are still active in our lives on a daily basis. Our family members in Heaven and our guardian angels are attentive to what's going on in our lives, including our wants, needs, and wishes. They see us. They know what we're going through. Although they do not eavesdrop on every thought and conversation, they are there for the important matters in our lives. But, sometimes, the most important events are those little moments that seem insignificant and mundane at the time.

Our precious and treasured moments with our deceased loved ones may not have taken place during the holidays or at large family gatherings. It was the funny catastrophes and unexpected debacles. The laughter during a home improvement project gone wrong. The personal connections and conversations and inside jokes. This is what we remember most about our loved ones in Heaven. And trust me, they are still with us every single week, keeping us company during our seemingly unimportant tasks, projects, and activities.

So, the next time you're making pancakes or having a garage sale, please have faith that you're not alone. Those who you miss the most are with you in spirit form, smiling, laughing, and watching over you. And if it's the spirit of your dad visiting while you're attempting to fix something, he's probably looking over your shoulder, making sure you're doing it the right way (the way he always did it).

What is Heaven like?

I know Heaven exists. In the fall of 2006, I had a very interesting experience. At the time, I was living in a two-bedroom apartment with a roommate. It was a Thursday night, and I went to bed a little early. Around three o'clock in the morning, I woke up out of a dead sleep. Lying on my back, I looked straight up at the ceiling. In the middle of my ceiling, there was a jagged cutout. A puzzle piece of missing ceiling that spanned a few feet in diameter.

Through this hole in my ceiling, I could see right through the top of my apartment into the high heavens. I was transfixed, looking at shining stars, swirling galaxies, and glowing planets, all the while still lying in my bed. I did a double take at first, thinking I was not yet fully awake or was hallucinating. I wasn't. I was wide awake. My thoughts were crystal clear, but my body felt strange. I didn't want to move, and I felt so comfortable that I probably couldn't have, even if I wanted to. The galaxy scene above me was indescribable in its splendor and beauty.

All of a sudden, God began speaking to me. The "voice" wasn't actually a voice at all. It was a *feeling*. Although hard to explain, the information being said to me from God in this experience was an instant transfer of thought.

I didn't hear it with my ears. I heard it with my heart. It was an instantaneous, telepathic transfer of thought and information.

What God "said" to me was that if I wanted all the answers to life's questions, all I had to do was float upwards, through my ceiling, and into the beautiful scene of galaxies above me. He said that if I wanted to be reunited with all of my loved ones in Heaven, be free of pain, absent of fear, and experience unimaginable peace, all I had to do was drift up, beyond the boundary of my ceiling and into the universe directly overhead.

I was sold. It sounded perfect. It felt like what I always imagined Heaven would feel like. I was ready to go and felt my spirit or my soul begin to rise upward from my bed and towards the glowing planets and twinkling stars.

The emotional and physical feelings I had during the whole experience were the most fantastic, indescribable part. I felt love. Pure, *unconditional* love. I felt enveloped in the softest, warmest, and most comforting embrace that I have ever encountered before. I felt free. I felt like my true self. In that moment, in that clarity of thought, I remembered who I really was. I felt an absence of fear. A complete and total lack of worry or anxiety of any kind. I was reminded that the soul cannot be damaged. *Ever.* I was reminded that our eternal spirit still contains a spark of the divine within it. I literally felt a pulse of love shooting through me like a heartbeat, getting more intense every second or two. *Thump thump. Thump thump.*

If you could take all of the best physical sensations you've felt and combine them together (all of the hot baths, the orgasms, the massages, the hugs, kisses, and feelings of relaxation), this is what I physically felt at that moment. A lifetime's worth of physical splendor experienced in one moment. In addition to the physical sensation, the emotional aspect was equally powerful. If you could take all the best moments you've ever emotionally experienced and condense them into one moment in time, this is the equivalent of what I felt as I floated up into the galaxy scene above me. Imagine hearing the words, "I love you," the birth of your first child, the exchange of your wedding vows, all the laughter, all the good memories and all the joy you've ever known, and imagine feeling this all at the same instant in time. It was a lifetime's worth of uncontrolled emotional and physical euphoria coursing through every cell of my body. It was love. Pure love.

Floating up to my ceiling on that brisk fall night, away from this world and towards the embrace of a loving God, I began to second guess my decision to "leave." I hesitated. A part of me wasn't quite ready. As much as I wanted to be freed from the confines of this hostile world, an inner knowing that I had unfinished business tugged at my soul. In that moment, through another instant transfer of thought, I told God I was not ready to leave this Earth after all. "I have too much work left to do and too many people still to help." I knew this was true. I knew it was not my time to go. It was my decision to make, and I made up my mind to stay on this Earth. Yet, there was still a part of me that yearned for whatever it was that waited beyond the boundaries of my bedroom ceiling, out in the vastness of space.

"I'm supposed to do something *big* in life, and I haven't done it yet. I'm not ready to go." As I "said" this to God, I felt a jolt. A twitch. A surge of blood rushing through my limbs. It was as if my soul snapped back into my physical body, like a rubber band stretched to its breaking point and then retracted. I looked around my room for a brief second, still on my back and lying on my bed. I gazed up to notice the hole in my ceiling was gone. The scene of swirling galaxies, glowing planets, and twinkling stars disappeared. As I stared at the textured, white ceiling of my bedroom, and took a deep breath, I wiped a tear from my cheek and sat up in bed.

I didn't sleep a wink for the rest of the night. In the depths of my soul, I knew that if I drifted off to sleep and was again presented with this opportunity from God, I would have taken it. The opportunity to "cross over" would have been too enticing to pass up a second time, and nobody would have ever known what happened to me or why I left this Earth. I question a lot of things in life, but I don't question whether this was a real experience. It was. It happened to me. And it changed my life forever.

Why did this happen? Why was I given the chance to leave? And if I really was about to depart this Earth, does that mean my body would have died, while my soul floated up through my ceiling? I don't know. At the time, I was told I had a fairly severe case of sleep apnea, which in some cases can be fatal. Perhaps, this was a classic near death experience.

Just a few months after this life-changing event, I began a new chapter in my life. A chapter of self-discovery and spiritual progress. I made many drastic changes in my life regarding my habits, my social life, my actions, and intentions. I cut ties with many draining individuals in my life at the time, which happened to be every single friend and acquaintance I had. I went through a period of soul searching, and read dozens of books related to spirituality. I began a chapter of isolation due to not having any friends. It was not a pity party. Rather, it was a time to collect myself and reinvent myself before my life became increasingly more meaningful. From that point on, I made a conscious effort to seek out individuals who would aid me on my spiritual journey, rather than hinder my progress. I began to surround myself with positive individuals, and within two years of that life-altering experience, I started to hone my intuitive skills by giving psychic readings.

I often think one of the "big things" I'm destined to do is write this book and other books in the future. Maybe, it involves giving lectures around the country and speaking my truth. I know it includes helping others, one person at a time, by using my intuition and trying to inspire them. Maybe these "big things" include all of the above. I'm passionate about providing people hope, validation, and peace of mind. My passion grows by the day. I have an insatiable appetite for helping others, and God willing, I will never, ever retire from this line of work that I love so much.

I feel gratitude for every breath, second chance, and life itself. And for the opportunity to do something important with my existence. That cosmic vision was a defining moment in my life, and it gave me hope. It made my purpose clearer than ever. It helped me to understand the extent to which we are capable of experiencing true happiness.

So, what is Heaven like? It's an ice cream cone on a hot July day. It's like our favorite song coming on the radio at just the perfect time. It's a cup of hot chocolate as we watch it snow outside. Heaven is the smell of a newborn baby as we hold her to our chests. It's lounging around the living room with loved ones after a bountiful Thanksgiving dinner and reminiscing about funny stories from the past. It's a warm blanket, fresh out of the dryer. It's a watercolor sunset in the distance that feels so close we could reach out and touch it. Heaven is looking into the eyes of our partner as we make love to them. It's the laughter at a birthday party and the celebration of life itself. It's all of these things wrapped up into a package so small that it can fit inside every cell of our bodies.

For a brief moment, I straddled the fence between Heaven and Earth, and I lived to tell my story. If the rest of Heaven is half as astounding as what I sampled, we are all in for a treat of unsurpassed splendor when we leave this Earth. Until then, we have much work left to do. We have *big* things to accomplish.

I'd like to think that there is no such thing as an insignificant moment in our lives. Maybe, we're all doing something *big* every moment of every day. I'd like to think so. And I'd like to think I learned this in that moment of clarity, one crisp fall night, lying in my bed and looking at Heaven through my bedroom ceiling.

How can I find more peace in my life?

If you were a child of the 60s and 70s, then *you* tell *me*. I've heard there was lots of peace, love, and funny things smoked in the back of vans during that era. Honestly though, the secret of life is not really in finding peace; it's about digging deeply enough to reach our own reservoir of joy that resides within us. We were born with all the happiness we'll ever need. Trust me. God essentially filled us up to the brim with happiness until we were about to overflow, and did so before we even entered this world.

Jubilation, bliss, and unimaginable elation are already inside of you. So, since you don't have to "find" peace, the question then becomes, "How do I dig through all the murky crap inside my spirit to find the happiness God placed inside of me?" Now that's a question worth talking about!

First of all, remember life is too short not to have fun. *All* of us are guilty of not having enough fun in life. What did you do today that brings you joy? What did you do as a kid that brought you joy that you don't do now as an adult? My sister colors in coloring books on a weekly basis for stress relief and simply because it's fun. Why don't we all allow ourselves to laugh more? Why can't we let our guards down more often and admit that it's hard work being so serious all the time? My mother-in-law hula-hoops in her living room. Just for the hell of it. Seriously. She's digging deep and making a conscious effort to reach her happiness. And you know what? Maybe, just maybe, she's found it.

Someday I'm going to write an entire book on how to be happy and find peace in our lives. For now, though, here are what I believe to be the secrets of life in one paragraph. Laugh until you cry. Blow bubbles. Skip. Spin in circles. Sing, even if you don't have the best voice in the world. Tell a joke. Ask someone else to tell *you* a joke. Color (outside the lines). Make a silly noise. Let your guard down. Let your hair down. Give someone a high five. For God's sake, have a slice of cake at the birthday party. So what if it goes straight to your thighs. You'll get newer, better thighs in your next lifetime anyway. Live in the moment. Let go of the past. Be optimistic about the future. Have no regrets. Know that you are perfect in your imperfections, and God wouldn't have you any other way.

If there is no such thing as Hell, then where do all the bad people go? How does God fit into all of this?

This one lady was pissed at me. I mean *pissed*. I was teaching a class at a community college on the subject of past lifetimes, and apparently I just pushed this woman's hot button. I stated my belief that there is no such thing as Hell, prepared to offer my explanation as to why I believe this, and I swear I saw steam start to come out of her nostrils before I could utter another word. "But, well, then how on Earth do you explain Hitler?" she asked. "And what about Osama Bin Laden? What happens to murderers and terrorists? You can't possibly think they actually go to Heaven!"

I understand that I'm going against the grain of thousands of years of religious teachings here, yet I stand unwavering in my intuitive truth. Hell does not exist. I'll use the Dalai Lama in a little analogy here. Because of his faith and spiritual obligations to promote peace, he's one of the most gentle souls the world has ever seen. He wouldn't hurt a fly (and I do mean that literally). The Dalai Lama respects everyone he comes in contact with and would never intentionally hurt another living being in any way, physically or emotionally. Even if someone wronged him or had ill-intent for him, the Dalai Lama does not have it within him to retaliate or seek vengeance.

Last time I checked, God loves us on a level we cannot fully comprehend. So, if the Dalai Lama loves all others and is incapable of hurting them, how then could God (who loves us even more than the Dalai Lama) have it within Him to sentence anyone to an eternity of torture and suffering in a burning inferno called Hell? Logic dictates that God wouldn't. Anyone who gives love on such a grand scale as God would never, under any circumstances, harm living beings, let alone torture them forever.

People like to talk about free will and how it enters into the equation of going to Hell or going to Heaven. It's our choice, right? Do good and get a ticket into Heaven. And those who do bad? Well, that was their choice. It was their free will. They made the wrong decision, and now they have to suffer the consequences, right? Using our heads and our intellect, this doesn't make sense either. It's not free will at all if a god says to us, "You can choose option A or you can choose option B. It's completely your choice (but choose option A or else you'll be punished)." That's not giving us a choice. That's giving us an ultimatum. It's manipulative and restricting.

First of all, if God wanted us all to be perfect, He would have created us to be perfect without any chance for us to make mistakes and disappoint Him. Secondly, the concept of praying your way into Heaven by going to church and worshiping God doesn't make sense either. What kind of self-absorbed egomaniac would create an entire species just for the sake of expecting them to grovel at his feet? Someone would have to be very insecure to need that kind of constant approval. God is not insecure. Being insecure is not a good quality. Since God is perfect in every sense of the word, He is not insecure. He does not need us to constantly worship Him and stroke His ego.

I have heard people quote the Bible by saying something to the equivalent of, "God is a jealous God and doesn't want us worshiping other deities." Even the First Commandment says something like this, right? Think about it intellectually. What could God possibly feel threatened by? What on Earth could God possibly be jealous of? God created everything. Therefore, if people are worshiping anything in the known universe, they are worshiping something that God Himself created. Why would He be threatened by this? He wouldn't. He would appreciate the fact that we were admiring His work, His creation.

Giving God human emotions does not make any sense, let alone attributing *petty* emotions to Him such as jealously, insecurity, and anger. God is perfect. You and I would both agree with this. A *perfect* being wouldn't exhibit negative personality traits of any kind. Therefore, I am led to believe that God is not angry with us. God is not violent and would not throw us into Hell for falling short of unrealistic expectations. Anger is a human emotion, not the emotion of an all-loving God. Besides, *He* is the one who gave us free will, so how could He possibly be mad at us for exercising our free will? God does not judge us.

God is not disappointed in us. He is proud of us for doing the best we can. When we are *not* doing the best we can, He understands that everything happens for a reason and has faith that we'll turn it all around. God would not threaten us with the possibility of Hell. Again, threatening someone would be a human characteristic of a person who is being manipulative and trying to get his own way.

Now, let's address all of those "bad" people. If they're not going to Hell, then what exactly happens to them? I'm going to ask you to keep an extremely open mind here and view this whole topic from a completely different angle, okay?

Rather than looking at a person's actions as "right" or "wrong," please view them in the context of what role the person is fulfilling in this lifetime. Think of life as one big cosmic community theater in which we're all playing a part. There are villains, heroes, love interests, people here for comic relief, and the plot is always changing. We all root for the hero in the play, don't we? I know I sure do. The person playing the role of hero at the community playhouse sure is fortunate, but in community theaters, the actors will want to challenge themselves and eventually take a turn playing different roles. In the future, the hero will eventually fulfill the role of villain and vice versa. Life is like a community theater. The "bad guys" in life are not going to Hell, but are simply fulfilling a role so that the heroes always have an adversary and obstacles to overcome.

How could there be heroes if there weren't villains? How could there be a happy ending if there were no trials and tribulations in the middle of the plot? If the play were made up of nothing but heroes experiencing nothing but easy times and peace, it would sure be a dud of a play. Boring enough to put us to sleep. If it were a movie, it would be one big, fat flop at the box office. The world needs "bad" people to keep us "good" people busy. The world needs chaos so we can work for peace. The world needs gang members, so there can be gang prevention counselors fulfilling their work of helping and being of service.

There need to be terrorists, so military units have the chance to strengthen their teamwork skills, discipline, and get the fulfillment of keeping their countries safe. The world has to have murderers so the grief counselors, investigators, clergymen, and social workers have something to do and someone in need of help. If they didn't have people to assist, then the grief counselors, investigators, clergymen, and social workers would not be able to accomplish their life purposes.

We're all fulfilling a role. You and I are simply getting the privilege of being the "good guys" in this particular lifetime. In past lifetimes, maybe we were *not* so good. As I've said before, the universe is a fair place, even though it doesn't always seem like it. We all eventually have to take a few turns playing the role of the bad guys so that others can work on stopping the crime, hate, chaos, and violence. This lets everyone feel what it's like to help, heal, protect, comfort, advocate, and attempt to spread love throughout the world.

Looking at it from this angle, those individuals who appeared to have a one-way ticket to Hell now appear to be more selfless and brave. They're not having much fun in this life, because they're too busy setting up opportunities for the rest of us to make the world a better place. Maybe, instead of condemning and judging "bad guys," we should say a silent prayer of thanks that they're making us look really good this time around and helping us to be the heroes. It's a lot more fun playing the role of "good guy" and "hero" than it is to be the villain.

My goal in this section was not to change your beliefs. I was simply answering the initial question with my heart, intellect, and intuition. These are *my* beliefs, and it's *my* truth. Maybe it's your truth now, and maybe it's not. I understand one chapter in one book cannot over-ride an entire lifetime of teachings and scriptures that were instilled in a person. It's not my job to change anyone's beliefs anyway. What matters is what *you* believe. Whatever you believe is *your* truth. And *your* truth is just as valid as *my* truth.

My cat, Darwin (the infamous Galloping Walrus of West Omaha), likes to lounge flat on his back with his head twisted to the side ever so slightly. He looks at me from that upside down position and seems to have a little twinkle of curiosity in his eyes. I think he does this because he finds it fun to view things from a different angle. A new perspective. Maybe it wouldn't hurt us to do the same, from time to time, even when it comes to our spiritual and religious beliefs. We can learn a lot from upside-down cats.

Does God use other people to deliver messages to us?

Let me tell you a story about a pirate sword and a circus. Before I began doing my intuitive work full time, I was a social worker. I've worked in nearly every human services environment imaginable. I've facilitated and organized sports programs and worked at summer camps. I've been employed at a group home, mentoring young men with behavioral issues, and I've logged countless hours at a day facility for adults suffering from mental illnesses. Once, I even taught a class about puberty and "personal changes" to a group of snickering adolescent boys in an after-school program. Doing so was about as difficult as holding onto a greased up watermelon on a rollercoaster ride. I definitely earned my paycheck that week.

While working for a facility that catered to adults affected by mental illnesses, I had the responsibility of taking a half dozen of our clients on an outing to the Shrine Circus. What a day! Chaos at every turn. There was confusion about which vehicle I was supposed to use to transport them. It was pandemonium at the Civic Auditorium as we pulled up and attempted to unload the van. Screaming kids everywhere! There were frazzled human services employees from all corners of the city frantically trying to keep their herds together as they traversed the cotton candy filled corridors inside the auditorium. Disarray. Turmoil. Bedlam. Needless to say, I was stressed.

My assembly of clients had just taken their respective seats in the audience, and just as the show began, Dorothy reported she had to use the restroom. Not wanting to leave my other clients all by themselves, and anxious that she may not be able to find the restroom in the winding hallways of the auditorium, I thought she should use the buddy system. I asked one of the responsible and intellectually high-functioning group members to help Dorothy find the restroom. My blood pressure was still through the roof, but for the time being, that particular fire was put out. Problem solved. "Please come right back guys, okay?"

Five minutes later, Dorothy and her navigating partner arrived back at our seats. Behind me, I heard a loud, raspy voice saying, "Pardon me. Excuse me. Comin' through. Sorry. Watch out now." I looked over my shoulder to see Dorothy ambling down the staircase towards our group with a six-foot-tall, oversized, inflatable pirate sword, and a smile on her face as wide as the Grand Canyon. She ungracefully plopped down in the seat right next to me, taking up nearly all of my leg room in the process. As I looked at her in disbelief, she whipped her head around to look me square in the face. She had a twinkle in her eyes that I had never seen before. A mischievous grin that symbolized the satisfaction in the purchase she had just made.

"Dorothy," I said, "Did you just buy yourself a giant pirate sword from one of the vendors in the hallway?"

Her smile grew even wider, and she replied, "Yep. Sure did. Had to get me one of these things."

So, there she was, a 55-year-old adult, sitting at the circus with her enormously humongous, inflatable pirate sword. She took a massive handful of popcorn and shoved it into her mouth, as she turned to face the juggling performance that was now taking place in the center ring.

I tipped my head and gazed upward at the sword in amazement. It stood resolute and incredibly tall. I then looked at the people in the row behind us, who were bobbing and weaving trying to see around the giant pirate sword so they could actually get a glimpse of the juggling act.

I looked back at Dorothy, as she was transfixed on the circus performers, holding her sword with one hand and eating her popcorn with the other. I thought to myself, "I get it now. I understand." Dorothy with her pirate sword not only helped me relax and enjoy the rest of the day, she helped me keep things in perspective. If she could enjoy her six-foot-tall, inflatable pirate sword and watch the circus with the wonder and amazement of an innocent child, then why on Earth couldn't I enjoy it, too? She wasn't the slightest bit stressed out. So, maybe, I didn't need to be either. Sometimes, we all take things too seriously. We forget to slow down and enjoy life's simple pleasures.

This is one of countless experiences when something happened at just the right time and place to teach me an important life lesson. Everything *does* happen for a reason. No significant moment happens by chance. Sometimes, God, the universe, or our guardian angels use people around us to deliver a message we need to hear. Did Dorothy realize she was teaching me a life lesson I would never forget? Did she recognize she was a messenger from God that day at the circus? Probably not. But I still considered her a popcorn-eating, pirate sword-wielding angel.

The world is in perfect sync. We all fit together like the intricate workings of a Swiss watch. Each one of us affects the others, and oftentimes, we are teaching and learning life lessons without even realizing it. Have an open mind, and keep an open heart. If something is supposed to happen, it will. If a message is supposed to be delivered to you, you'll get it, one way or another. Even if it's at the circus and delivered from Dorothy.

Which religion is the right one?

If we asked three people to identify the color of a living room wall, it's very possible that we would get three different interpretations. Beige. Tan. Light brown. Which one is correct? All of them? Or, maybe, none of them, if you ask a fourth person who calls it cappuccino. The person who calls it beige could accuse the person calling it tan of being color blind. The person who believes the wall is tan can therefore accuse the "beige" person of being color blind. Person number three would say they're both off base and don't have an eye for color in the first place. Each of these three people are all having the same problem in that they cannot view the wall color from the exact same perspective of the other two. Therefore, there is no way to determine who is right and who is wrong.

It's a matter of perspective and opinion. They could try asking the wall, but this would cause further frustration when the wall doesn't answer them. In truth, the wall probably does not care what label the three people give it. The wall is simply happy that the three people are looking at it and appreciating its color, whatever color it really is.

If this little philosophical analogy I've concocted doesn't quite do it for you, let's think about this as rational, logical adults. There cannot be one "right" religion, because that would imply there are "wrong" religions. If you assume someone choosing the wrong religion would therefore be denied entrance into Heaven, then justice and fairness no longer exist within the universe. I say this because it would take a cruel and scandalous god to deny a person access into Heaven for not following the "right" religion, when the "right" religion may not have even been present in that person's part of the world.

Perhaps, they had never even heard of Jesus, let alone been given a chance to attend a Christian church or read the Bible. If a person is of the belief that Christianity is the one and only path that leads to Heaven, it would not be fair to those other five billion people on Earth who subscribe to a different belief system.

If the Hindu's have it "right," then should the two billion Christians curse their darned bad luck for not being born in India? Of course not. The world is a fair place, and God is a fair God. We generally tend to follow the spiritual teachings that are most accepted by our friends, family, and members of society in whatever part of the world we happen to grow up. We will all be accepted at the pearly gates. Saint Peter will not be standing there with his checklist in hand, waving people through who happened to be lucky enough to follow the "right" religion because it was prevalent in the part of the world they lived in; whereas, the next person would be turned away because the "truth" was not preached in their culture.

You have to admit that would be a pretty random admittance into Paradise, wouldn't it? I think God gave us a golden, round-trip ticket before we even entered into this world. He told us that we're free to choose whatever winding, bumpy, twisting path we want while on this Earth, but all roads lead back to Him. All roads lead back to Heaven. In case you lose your ticket, don't worry. God has you on the guest list, no matter which faith you follow.

Andy, what are your religious beliefs?

I don't have any, per se. I am not a religious person. I am a spiritual person. What's the difference? I guess that depends on which minister, philosopher, or bartender you ask. You'll probably get a different answer from every person on the subject of spirituality or religion. In my eyes, spirituality is more of a personal connection with God, and religion is more of a formal relationship. Spirituality is free-flowing and does not contain any laws, rules, or regulations. Religion has a fairly rigid set of expectations and beliefs. Religion has parameters between which its followers are strongly suggested to live. Spirituality has no parameters and no limits except those that you put on yourself.

I once had a deep conversation with a co-worker. Super nice lady who would bend over backwards for anyone. She felt like everyone's sweet grandma. She happened to be *very* religious. We were talking about God and spirituality one morning, while we served up breakfast to the clients at the mental health facility where we worked. She couldn't quite wrap her head around the fact that I was a big believer in God and a big believer in morals, ethics, doing the right thing, and putting the needs of others first, but I did not adhere to Christianity or any formal religion.

She asked me, "Well, then, who do you pray to?"

With a puzzled look on my face, I lowered my voice to almost a whisper, thinking the conversation was getting too deep for our clients to overhear. I said, "Um, God. Who else would I pray to?"

She looked at me for a couple seconds and pondered my answer. I looked at her. She looked at me. A hint of a smile started to form around the edges of her mouth, and she replied, "Well, okay then." We went back to handing out bagels and juice to the clients.

Who else would I pray to? Many of us are taking different roads in getting to the same spiritual destination. Sometimes, I like to think of various religions as separate trails that wrap around the edges of a lake and converge at the same spot on the other side. Spirituality (my path) goes straight through the lake itself. My route takes me from log to log, as I bounce and swim across. I'll get to the other side of the lake just the same as the person who took the side road. My method in getting to the other side may not be a straight line, but I'll get there eventually, and I'm in no hurry.

I believe in God. I believe in the karmic circle of what goes around comes around. I believe that if we take care of those in need, we will be taken care of in *our* time of need. I believe that everything happens for a reason. I know the world is an organized place and even though it seems cruel and unfair at times, it's really not. I don't believe in Hell. I *do* believe that some of us have been through our own personal Hell on Earth and will do whatever exercises for the soul it takes to avoid going back to that dark, personal place.

I can't help but believe there is a little bit of good in everyone, and even those who appear to be lacking one, single, positive attribute, well, I have faith there's some good in them too. Somewhere deep down. I believe we are perfect in our imperfection, and I think God would agree with this. I feel whatever faith, religion, and personal set of values you live by is okay as long as it makes you a better person and doesn't hurt anyone else in the process. I believe a higher power hears all of our prayers and answers them, but only if it's in *everyone's* best interest to do so. I believe we are all here for a reason, and learning to love one another is at the top of that list. I believe God has the most wonderful sense of humor, and I figure I better have one, too, if I'm going to survive this journey called life.

Chapter 3: Love, Life, and Lucky Pennies

Are there such things as soul mates?
And if so, how do I know I'm with mine?

I hate to be so straightforward and blunt here, but if you have to ask the question, "Is my significant other my one true soul mate," then he/she is probably not. If he was, you wouldn't have to ask the question. You'd feel it in your heart of hearts, and as a matter of fact, you would know it to be true almost instantly when you first met him. I am a romantic, and it pains me to admit what I'm about to say about love.

Love isn't always about finding your soul mate. Sometimes, it's about finding someone with whom you are compatible, who treats you well, and who helps make life enjoyable for you. The person who fits that description may or may not be your soul mate, but if he's a great match for you, stick with him and enjoy the ride. Love is about compatibility. Love is also about timing. Just because you're ready to find Mr. Right doesn't mean he's in a convenient part of his life and ready to be with you. Maybe, he's in a messy relationship of his own right now. It's conceivable that he has some personal issues to work through until his path crosses your path on some fateful day in the future.

Love is sometimes about geography. Is your compatible person even in the same zip code or general geographic vicinity as you are? It may be driving cupid just as crazy as you that you're in the wrong place at the wrong time. I don't want to paint the picture that all the stars have to be perfectly aligned for you to find true love, but all of these factors do play a part.

So, what is a soul mate? It's your *perfect* match. Your complimentary balance. The yin to your yang, the up to your down, the creamer to your coffee, and the peanut butter to your jelly. Your soul mate is your best friend of all best friends. And I'm not just talking about this lifetime. I'm talking about the strongest bond you've ever had with anyone, anywhere, anytime in the history of your infinite existence. You see a lot of yourself in your soul mate. Your soul reflects in the twinkle of his eye, and he can finish your sentences before you've even said a word. You'll not only have a preposterous amount of things in common with your soul mate, but the areas in which you differ will cause you to balance each other out so perfectly that it will appear as if a cosmic teeter totter is stuck in the horizontal position with you on one side and your partner on the other. Perfect balance. Perfect love.

Due to the immense number of lifetimes we live and the fact that the world is such a big place, we don't often incarnate with our soul mate at the same point in time. Even when we do, our paths don't typically tend to cross due to geographic reasons. To have your one and only soul mate on this Earth and in your life is incredibly rare. My advice to you is this: Spend a little less time worrying about your soul mate and a little more time looking for red flags in the beginning stages of your relationships.

Don't sell yourself short, and don't settle for someone who is good for you when you have the possibility of being with someone who is *great* for you. I have met countless individuals who were not with their one and only soul mate, but were in a completely happy, healthy, and long-lasting relationship that brought joy for each person on an unimaginable scale. I can't emphasize this enough. Just because you may not be with your soul mate, it *doesn't* take an ounce of specialness out of your relationship.

Does he treat you right? Are you attracted to him emotionally, physically, and intellectually? Does he accept you for who you are? For God's sake, does he make you laugh? I hope so. Looks will fade, but personalities tend to last. Hold on to the one you love, whether he's your soul mate or not. If he makes you happy, and you also give joy back to him, it may just be the right relationship for you.

If you are one of the lucky few who have met your soul mate during this particular incarnation here on Earth, then enjoy! I have noticed an interesting trend over my years of giving readings. Soul mates often wait until their last incarnations to live a lifetime with one another on Earth. Having the rare experience of being with your soul mate here on Earth must be the "graduation present" from God for making it to our last lifetime. In terms of love, this is the grandest example of saving the best for last.

How do I know if I'm "on track" in my life?

If you're on track, you'll be happy. If you're on track, you'll feel fulfillment in your life. If you're on track, you won't mind rolling your weary bones out of bed when your alarm goes off in the morning. When we're staying true to the life course we're supposed to be on, we tend to function out of a slightly higher level of consciousness. This means you'd be able to not only take care of yourself but would have a little extra energy left over to be of service to others and help *them* find some happiness of their own.

When you're on track, you'll feel a wonderful and nagging sense of déjà-vu. Why this happens will be explained more thoroughly in the chapter on reincarnation. Life will feel so familiar when you're on track, because you pre-planned this life path before you entered into this world. Writing our own script of life is something we do with the help of our spirit guides before we arrive here as infants. As adults, we go through the motions and act out the play we wrote for ourselves, which then causes feelings of familiarity and déjà-vu.

Simply asking yourself whether or not you're on track is a good sign that you *are*. Those who are off track may never stop to ask themselves that question or take stock in their personal/spiritual progress. Believe it or not, your life is probably going according to plan. Are you going to make mistakes in life? As sure as the sky is blue, yes, you will. Good God Almighty, have I made some mistakes myself. Some whoppers, in fact! But just because we've made mistakes in the past and may continue to have a little life hiccup here or there doesn't mean we are derailed from the tracks we're meant to follow.

Sometimes being "on track" is a matter of perspective. We're typically not an accurate judge of ourselves when it comes to this matter. Furthermore, we often don't give ourselves enough credit even when we *are* on track. Regarding perspective and staying on track, here's a little analogy. If you've ever flown on an airplane, you'll agree that the landscape below seems to be moving pretty darn slowly. Cars on the highway look like they're practically standing still, even though they're moving around sixty miles per hour. Rivers, forests, and other geographic markers seem to be frozen in time, making it feel like the airplane you're in is not going very fast. But it's all about perspective. From your seat, it's hard to gauge just how fast the aircraft is moving. If you were able to step outside your window, you'd be blown away (literally) by just how fast the plane is flying through the sky. Since we are often blinded by our own point of view, please know that you are probably making faster spiritual and personal growth than you realize. You most likely *are* on track and are cruising right along at an amazing speed.

I want you to repeat something for me. "I am the captain of my own ship. Mistakes only make me stronger. Each time I've gotten lost, I've found my way back to my true

North. My path may be a winding one, but I WILL get to the end, one way or another. I am on track. I am guided. I will stay focused on the journey, not the destination."

How can I be a better partner for my significant other, and how can I do a better job of showing affection?

How do you currently say "I love you" to the special person in your life? Do you make sure the dishes are always promptly done? If it infuriates your partner to have last night's lasagna caked to the bottom of the dish like dried concrete, then I'd say that's the smartest way of showing you care. Do you simply verbalize affection to your partner by saying, "I love you?" Maybe, you're good at giving him compliments and telling him he's handsome, even as he lays in bed with morning breath and frazzled hair at 6:00 a.m. Perhaps, you show him physical affection by showering him in hugs, kisses, and gently scratching his back, as you both sit on the couch watching a movie.

I'm asking these questions because people tend to *give* affection in the same way they wish to *receive* it. I didn't come up with this marriage-saving idea. It's proven, factual research that has been done by *actual* doctors of love. Therefore, if you want *your* back rubbed, you're likely to rub your partner's back. If you wish your spouse would be more of a "doer" and go out of his or her way to take out the trash, finish the laundry, or pick up the groceries, *you're* likely to be doing these things for *them*. This is fine, and there's nothing wrong with it, per se. However, the one mistake a lot of couples make is they get into the habit of showing affection to their partner in ONLY one way (the way in which they hope to receive affection).

Let's talk about exercising and a term called "muscle confusion." It's a fact that our bodies are smart and can adapt to exercise very quickly. It's also a fact that if you train for months on end doing the exact same exercise again and again, your muscles are smart enough to adjust to this. When your body expects it, your muscles are no longer challenged by it, therefore, you don't burn as many calories doing the exercise as you used to. It's old news. It's not stimulating for your body anymore. Showing affection in your relationship is very similar. You must mix it up a bit. As the saying goes, "Variety is the spice of life." I'll take that a step further and say, "Variety can really spice up your love life."

This month, continue keeping a clean house for your partner. She will appreciate it and appreciate *you* for being conscientious enough to pick up after yourself. Next month, maybe you could work on expressing *words* of affection by giving your partner genuine and unexpected compliments. The month after that, perhaps, you can concentrate on surprising your significant other with little gifts. It doesn't have to be a new car, but simple little things that say, "I love you." Start with an affordable bouquet of flowers or a nice greeting card and go from there. If you have a creative bone in your body, you may even want to *make* one of these with your own two hands. Writing a little poem may have a big impact. Even if you're not the most articulate person on the planet, I'm sure your partner would still appreciate the effort. Mix it up! Shake up your routine. My wife and I sometimes drive around town until we find a restaurant we've never tried. Something as simple as a new environment or new activity can be all it takes for the sparks to start flying in any relationship.

Lastly, I want to suggest you keep your motives unselfish. True love does not mean doing these things for your partner simply because you want something in return. Don't be thinking about yourself when you're doing these acts of kindness for the person you care about. Remember, what goes around comes around. Trust the universe, and know when the time is right, you'll be spoiled in return.

Is there any proof behind the theory that our lives are pre-planned before we're born?

Carpenters and others who work with their hands have a saying that goes, "Measure twice, cut once." This basically means a person will save themselves a little time and effort by planning more thoroughly before doing the actual work. Personally, I will admit I've not always followed that logic. I usually end up measuring once, cutting three times, measuring again only to find out I was wrong the first time, cut again, throw the hammer, drop the saw, then call someone who knows what they're doing to salvage what's left of my fix-it project. My point, though, is when we plan ahead, strategize, and methodically plan out what we're going to do before we do it, there are generally good results.

Our lives work in much the same way. There are

numerous reasons why we all plan out our lives before we live them. First of all, if we came into this wild and wooly world without a road map, we'd run a very serious risk of getting lost. On a long road trip, for example, you reduce the risk of getting lost if you have a map or, better yet, GPS. Secondly, we plan our lives before coming into this world, so we'll have the opportunity to work on specific lessons. For example, if you're coming into this particular lifetime to work on your social skills, it wouldn't make any sense to be down in a remote corner of the world having no other people with whom to interact. You would most likely plan to live in a big city or at least to have plenty of opportunities to meet new people.

Planning out our lifetime before we live it just makes sense. You get more bang for your buck if you're prepared. Poor planning or no planning whatsoever typically causes poor results. If you go to the grocery store unprepared, without a list, you'll not only wander around the store longer than you hoped, but you'll leave with random items you didn't initially need. Trust me. A bag of cheese doodles and a king-sized candy bar says I'm right.

Being prepared translates to being more efficient. When a person is more efficient, more is accomplished. When a person accomplishes more in life, he gains more experience and wisdom. It's because we are eternal beings that we are able to plan our lives before we're born. If you believe we are still alive after we die, then logic dictates we were already alive before we were born. When you view it this way, life suddenly seems much more cyclical rather than linear. I want to share a couple of stories with you that may provide a little validation to the fact we pre-plan our life journey.

I gave an intuitive reading to a lady I'll call Sharon. We were talking about her family and loved ones, but suddenly, we found ourselves talking about her pets. She told me she had a dog. It popped into my head that her dog was an eight-year-old pug, and I verbalized this to her. She cocked her head and through squinted eyes asked me, "How on Earth did you know that?"

I winked at her and said, "Maybe I should look into being a professional psychic." We had a good laugh together. Although intuitively knowing the exact age and breed of Sharon's dog may not make front page news, it indeed has everything to do with the fact that our lives are pre-planned. The reason I knew Sharon had an eight-year-old pug is because it was written into her life chart long ago that at this point in time she was *supposed* to have an eight-year-old pug. The fact this was accurate just showed Sharon was on track, experiencing exactly what she came here to experience.

In another session, I met with a nice lady named Becky who briefly mentioned her upbringing in various Catholic churches. I interrupted her in mid-sentence to ask if she had any ties to Milwaukee, Wisconsin. She smiled and nodded her head, as she revealed to me that she attended many Catholic churches in Milwaukee because she lived there for the first twenty years of her life. Again, she *planned* to live in Milwaukee for the first twenty years of her life and be raised Catholic long before she was even a twinkle in her daddy's eyes. It was written into Becky's life chart; therefore, it was intuitively spelled out in black and white for me.

While meeting with another client, Danielle, I mentioned at some point in her life she'd have the opportunity to go to the country of Tunisia. Although this message was seemingly far-fetched, she told me she had recently been in contact with a business associate of hers who was doing work in Tunisia, and her friend wanted Danielle to visit. Whether or not she'll ever take the opportunity is still up in the air. That's dictated by her free will. It was merely written into Danielle's life script that the opportunity would be *presented* to her. She is on track and living out the plan she made for herself long ago.

In yet another reading, I told Allison she would be given the chance to play a nurturing/mentoring role to a boy named Teagan. It made no sense to her at the time. However, after going home and talking to her husband about our reading, she got back to me and said the message made complete sense. Allison's husband told her he just found out that his friends from California were moving back to town. They have a little boy named Teagan, and her husband was excited for their families to spend a lot of time together in the coming years. I'm not sure what lessons Allison is supposed to teach Teagan in the future, but I know she'll get the chance, just as it was written into her life path long before Allison entered into this lifetime.

Everything tends to go according to plan. Whether it's

having the pet you were always destined to have, traveling to places you were meant to see, or crossing paths with the right person at the right time, we all are living out the script to a play we wrote in Heaven before coming to Earth.

Can some people be cursed with bad luck?
Do curses and spells exist?

Athletes are superstitious. They'll do any old ritual, however odd, to give them a competitive edge against their opponents. I have played soccer since I was six years old. When I was almost a teenager, I decided to wear a t-shirt underneath my jersey to absorb the sweat. I scored a goal while wearing this undershirt for the very first time and instantly decided this new undershirt was lucky. I wore that particular undershirt for so many years, in so many games, it became stained with sweat. It often smelled so bad it could be compared to the inside of a sweaty sailor's boot in the summertime. Nasty stuff! Biohazard level 4 material! Was it really lucky? Did it really give me an edge?

As the years went by and I gained a little more perspective about life and how the world works, I admitted it probably did nothing to make the soccer gods favor me any more than my opponents. Nowadays, I am not a superstitious person whatsoever. I know God is not playing favorites and giving me any more luck than the next person. I believe special powers reside within *ourselves*, not within the putrid, reeking funk of an old t-shirt. We make our own luck.

It's been verified through many psychological tests that people who claim to be "lucky" are simply more attentive and aware of the opportunities life presents them. They are more aware of the chances that pop up in their lives and are less hesitant to jump on new opportunities. People who describe themselves as "unlucky" in psychological experiments are found to simply be less observant and pass up many opportunities to better their day, such as finding a $20 bill on the sidewalk. They were no more "unlucky" than the next person, but their self-defeating attitude caused them to mope around feeling sorry for themselves instead of seizing the day.

I'm not saying to throw out all your lucky rabbit feet, auspicious coins, and blessed knick-knacks you've acquired throughout the years. After all, objects are just about as powerful as you believe them to be. If you believe your lucky coin will cause you to have a good day, then maybe it will. Just keep in mind the good fortune coming your way may have more to do with your expectations and positive thinking rather than the actual coin itself.

As a psychic medium, part of what I offer my clients is the ability to connect with their loved ones in Heaven. I provide validation that their loved ones are still very much alive and active on the Other Side. I'll never forget the reading I gave to a nice young lady named Carrie who was looking for some confirmation that her grandma had crossed over and was doing well in Heaven. I told Carrie, "She's doing great, but she keeps telling me something about pennies. She wants me to bring up lucky pennies, as if they had special meaning to the family. What is this about?"

Carrie's eyes welled with tears, and she explained how her grandmother had an unusual tendency to wear a penny inside her shoe as she went about her daily business. Although this sounded like it would be rather uncomfortable on her feet, Carrie's grandma found it to be good luck having a penny inside her shoe. Carrie then told me that all of her family members wore pennies inside their shoes when they attended Grandma's funeral service, in tribute to her. Lucky pennies or not, you have to love grandmothers for their loveable quirks and endearing habits.

Will there ever be world peace?

During his days in the White House, Ronald Reagan was quoted several times, essentially saying the same thing, "If alien intruders from outer space suddenly invaded our planet, our international wars and political differences would be put aside to fight together for a common cause." Although his wife's "Just Say No" campaign in the war against drugs was a huge flop, I think Reagan was really onto something with his alien talk. The world *would* come together if we had to defend ourselves and our planet against invaders from far away galaxies. The color of people's skin, what religion they practiced, and their political beliefs would suddenly become irrelevant, as we united with all of our brothers and sisters of humanity. In a way, an alien invasion could possibly be the best thing that ever happens to us.

Unfortunately, E.T. may not make his or her official appearance for quite some time. Until that happens, we will most likely continue to wage war against each other in frightening and technologically-advanced ways. Is world peace a realistic goal? Or is it more of a wish? Can it even be attained?

When I was young and already a little bit of a philosopher, I thought about this a lot. I prayed for it sometimes, too. Why do some countries have to invade others? What's with all this "conquer and divide" stuff? Can't people just open up their borders and share their resources, so there's enough to go around and plenty for everyone? I'm sure my innocent and naïve prayer was heard, but for reasons I'm just now starting to understand, the prayer may continue to go unanswered.

Remember back in the section where we talked about Hell and people fulfilling the good guy, bad guy roles? This constant struggle of good and evil makes the merry-go-round of life continue to spin. The plot becomes thicker by the year. We are living in scary times. Maybe the scariest and most uncertain in the history of our fragile planet.

However, if everything was perfect, peaceful, and harmonious, what would be the point of being here? Perfect peace is what we bask in while we're in Heaven. On the Other Side there are no struggles. There is no heartache and no fear. There is no war, famine, disease, or destruction, and no opportunities to make a bad situation better. We only get the chance to put a positive stamp on life while we're here in this frenzied environment.

World peace may sound like the solution to all our problems. Conversely, it would rob us of the opportunity to work on lessons, objectives, life goals, and make forward spiritual progress. Let's all remember what our peace-promoting friend Gandhi said, "You must *be* the change you wish to see in the world."

How can I be more tolerant of people who irritate me, and should I feel guilty for finding it hard to love people whom I don't even *like*?

Is there someone in your life who really pushes your buttons? Someone who makes you as grumpy as a T-Rex with a poison ivy rash? Some people just rub us the wrong way, don't they? Interacting with them feels like sandpaper on a sunburn! Rest assured, you don't have to like everyone. There is no universal law that says you must. One of the beautiful things about life is the diversity of our personalities.

Whether it's smacking your gum loud and clear for all to hear or biting your finger nails, we all have our nasty habits that make up our wonderful uniqueness. Nobody's perfect. Although we accept the fact that everyone has their flaws, we still occasionally get annoyed by others. Why is this?

One reason is because we are not in control of what others do. If that "jackass" steals the parking spot you had your eye on, there's not much you can do about it except mumble some creative profanity and find another parking space. If the child behind you in the airplane continues to kick the back of your seat with the power of a 3.4 magnitude earthquake, there's not much you can do about it besides politely ask the parents to have them stop it. But you know this will only buy you thirty seconds of sanity before the little soccer player behind you is back at it again.

We are not always in control. And it drives us nuts. The person who obnoxiously talks throughout the movie and ruins it for everyone else in their general vicinity is not likely to pay much attention when you ask them to pipe down. People get on our nerves because they have their own minds, their own free will, and the power to make their own decisions, which may contradict what we want them to do.

There are many more reasons we find it hard to love unconditionally, let alone *like* everyone we come in contact with. It's sometimes hard to view things from another person's perspective. It's difficult to put ourselves in other people's shoes, especially if we are irritated by their very presence. Why do they do the things they do? Perhaps, only God and the person's spirit guides can answer that question. Most importantly, you have to ask yourself, "What am I in control of?" The answer is, "Myself. Only myself."

People are stuck in their ways, and for the most part, they are who they are. They're not going to change. If they're not going to change, then we have no option but to change the way we perceive others and react to them. Breathe deeply, and sleep well, knowing God is not expecting you to like everyone or to be their best friend. If you can muster up the gumption to silently wish them well and recognize there is a piece of God somewhere deep within them, I would say you're doing pretty well at learning unconditional love.

Do our loved ones in Heaven make it to our special life events?

Of course, they do. They wouldn't miss it for the world. Since they watch us on a daily basis, they know what's going on in our lives. Trust me; they secured their spot with an RSVP long before you ever sent out the invitation. They will be there in spirit, whether it's the birth of your child, your parents' 40th wedding anniversary, a graduation, or a Bar Mitzvah. Mazel Tov! Although all of our loved ones keep a very busy and active schedule on the Other Side doing the activities they love, they are never too busy to attend the big events and special occasions in our lives.

I remember giving a reading to a young client of mine named Mandy, who was elated because she was a new mother, but saddened by the fact that *her* mother recently died and was not around on the day the baby was delivered. "Oh, but she *was* around," I told Mandy. Her deceased mother wanted me to tell Mandy that she was there in spirit, holding her hand all day long in the delivery room.

This made sense to Mandy, who then told me one of her hands was extraordinarily warm all day and she occasionally felt a slight pressure, as if someone was giving it a squeeze. At the time, she thought it was just her imagination. Her mom also wanted me to mention the new baby was named after a grandma. Mandy conceded she did name her new baby girl after a grandma, her maternal grandmother to be exact. A little validation can go a long way in knowing our loved ones *are* there in spirit for our big day, whatever the event may be.

On another occasion, I gave a medium reading to a spunky lady named Donna who wanted to know if her dad was pleased with the funeral service they gave him. By the way, they always are. They don't care whether we pick out red flowers or white flowers for their service. They'll be happy with whatever headstone you choose. They'll think it's wonderful if you choose to spread their ashes at sea, plant them under a willow tree, or shoot them out of a cannon. They love it! And they love you simply for taking the time to plan the service even though you're in a grief-filled fog.

Back to Donna, she wanted to know if her dad approved of the service. He not only approved, but he wanted me to bring up rainbows, telling me they had significance regarding his funeral service. Donna's tears of pain started turning into tears of joy, as she laughed and said, "Now that I think about it, it rained on the day of his funeral, and there was a double rainbow in the sky." Apparently dad was there. And he saw the rainbows.

Our loved ones in Heaven attend the big occasions in our lives. They are at the weddings. They are at the funerals. They are at the births and birthday parties. And they're present for Christmas, as well. One of my clients, Travis, lost his father. During the reading, I could feel his dad had a great sense of humor and loved to joke around. Travis' dad wanted me to bring up the fact that the previous Christmas, there were some presents that were misplaced or lost in the hustle and bustle of their family Christmas parties. Travis' dad told me the presents were not found or distributed to their respective recipients until well after Christmas passed.

Travis whispered, "Holy cow," and with a stunned look on his face, he proceeded to tell me his dad was correct. The previous Christmas, there were a few presents intended to be given to Travis' kids, and the gifts somehow were misplaced. It wasn't until a few days into the New Year that he found the gifts and gave them to his children. This message from his father was all the proof Travis needed to believe dad would be there for all the holidays and family functions in the future.

I have heard of the term "kindred spirit" before, but what does it mean?

A kindred spirit is a person who "gets you." It's a friend who is near and dear to your heart. It's the person who instinctively gives you all the black olives from their salad when you're at a restaurant, because they know you love black olives. It's the friend who intuitively knows you had a bad day and offers to watch the kids for a few hours so you can have some peace and quiet. It's the friend who accepts you, flaws and all. It's the friend with whom you have an unspoken bond. It's a person you can talk with until the sun comes up. The friend who you adore and lean on and forgive (even though she kissed your boyfriend freshman year and lied about it).

We all have at least one of these special individuals in our lives, don't we? Let me be clear about something though. A kindred spirit is not the same as a soul mate. However, this doesn't take away from the uniqueness of the relationship. So why would your bond be so strong with a kindred spirit? Because a kindred spirit refers to a connection that goes beyond this lifetime. A kindred spirit is an individual with whom you have spent plenty of time over in Heaven (in-between lifetimes).

The transitional time we spend in Heaven prior to and after our lifetimes on Earth is when many friendships are formed. Since a kindred spirit is not the same as a soul mate, you can have more than one kindred spirit. In fact, I'm sure you have several. Some of yours are here on Earth, right now, very much active in your life. Some of them are still in Heaven, awaiting your return or getting ready to reincarnate soon themselves.

I feel like I'm not living up to my true potential. Why is this?

If I had ever met Mother Teresa, she and I would have agreed that our spiritual philosophies and ideas on religion differ a bit. However, she hit the nail on the head with one particular quote, and it's something we should all keep in mind when we're talking about our potential. "We cannot do great things on this Earth, only small things with great love." The simple elegance and wisdom in that one sentence should take the weight of the world off our weary shoulders.

"Why am I not living up to my potential?" "I feel like I'm supposed to be doing something important with my life." "I know I'm destined to do big things, but why can't I figure out what those big things are?" I hear this from people all the time. Heck, in the past I've made similar statements myself. I know a lot of individuals who believe that God has a plan for them, but they just can't seem to figure out what that plan is. I believe that God's plan *is* your plan. Your plan *is* God's plan. I've said it before, and I'll say it again: Although our lives were pre-planned (by us) before we came into the world, there is still a lot of free will involved. Create life the way you want it to be. It's never too late to start doing little things with great love.

Please keep in mind that our view of ourselves is often skewed by perspective. People's opinions about themselves are generally not the opinions others have about them. If we're too close to a situation, we cannot act as an unbiased observer. It's like a person not knowing he is in the eye of a hurricane, because he is too close to the situation. It's all about perspective. If all this is true, then you are probably *already* living up to your true potential, but you just don't realize it. We're all more critical of ourselves than we need to be.

When talking about reaching our potential and feeling a sense of fulfillment, part of the problem is we don't stop often enough to give ourselves a pat on the back for small accomplishments and achievements. If you are suffering through a depression and are able to dress yourself in something *other than* your bathrobe, then congratulations! What an achievement! I say this without a hint of sarcasm. It's an accomplishment in itself to "dress for success when you're feeling depressed" (quote me on that one). If you can manage to do your hair and report to work on top of this, it's icing on the cake. It's extra credit. Bonus points. It's a lesson in perseverance and positive thinking, and in the eyes of your spirit guides and God Almighty, you just passed with an "A+."

If you are exhausted and somehow dig deeply enough into your well of self-discipline to get up before the sunrise and walk a mile on the treadmill, then in my opinion, that's worthy of a big golden trophy, my friend. You should view that as not only reaching your true potential but exceeding all expectations. If we focus on the here and now, keep things in perspective, and chip away at life's difficulties, little by little, we will reach our true potential.

Some people struggle more than others when it comes to finding happiness and feeling like they're living up to their true potential. If these challenges have led you to become chronically depressed, I would strongly encourage you to seek professional help from a qualified mental health professional. Seeking assistance for depression does not indicate that you are weak or vulnerable. Please don't let it damage your pride. In fact, letting your guard down and seeking help is actually a sign of wisdom, maturity, and growth.

I have known countless individuals from all walks of life who sought help from a therapist during rough chapters in their lives. With the help of anti-depressants, counseling, or both, nearly all of these people went on to make full recoveries and once again found the happiness they deserved. The importance of mental health professionals cannot be underestimated when it comes to our emotional well-being. If chronic depression, anxiety, and self-esteem issues have you feeling stuck, please take action and consult with a mental health practitioner. The social worker in me wants to remind you that seeking help from a counselor does *not* make you crazy. What's crazy is living in a state of depression and not taking action to correct the problem.

Why is the divorce rate so high these days?

Because husbands watch too much football on the weekend instead of taking their wives out on dates. Husbands out there may score touchdowns of a different kind (wink) if they took their wives out for a nice dinner, instead of lying on the couch, yelling at the T.V. because their team needs a new quarterback. Actually, I'm just being facetious. Whether a husband's fantasy football team is doing well or not, the fact remains the divorce rate has skyrocketed faster than Berkshire Hathaway stock. Why is this? Well, in my opinion, it's *not* because the world is "going to Hell in a hand basket." Intuitively, I believe there are two reasons why marriages don't seem to last like they used to.

The first reason is due to the human species evolving and becoming efficient students of life. Nowadays, there is an abundance of older, wiser souls walking the planet. As a civilization, we have not only evolved to live in a fast-paced world, we have grown to be fast learners as well. Translated to our conversation on divorce, this has huge implications, and it partially explains why married couples can't seem to stay together. Since we are all fast learners, it no longer takes us decades to learn from and grow with our spouse, as it did in generations past.

This could be seen as a good thing or a bad thing. I believe it's somewhere in the middle. It simply is what it is. A married couple is supposed to learn from and grow with each other in areas, such as, communication, trust, boundaries, intimacy, teamwork, parenting, loyalty, and forgiveness. It used to take several decades to accomplish all this, but now, it's taking much less time. I know there are some people who view this as a negative thing, but it's similar to high school students graduating early because they blew through the curriculum very quickly and racked up enough credits to graduate earlier than their peers. We would not condemn those students for being more advanced, would we?

The second reason I believe divorce courtrooms are busier than a sports bar on Super Bowl Sunday is because social media is causing this world to operate at a blistering speed. With social media and technology, we absorb and transfer information at the speed of thought. We are essentially packing more experiences and interactions into our daily lives, including our marriages. Busier lives translate to busier marriages, and all the life experiences couples are supposed to go through together are often packed into less than a decade. The expiration date of a marriage is the point at which a couple has nothing left to teach each other regarding trust, communications, boundaries, intimacy, compromise, and patience.

I'm not advocating a husband leave his wife tomorrow, because she accidentally washed his lucky jersey. And I'm not saying a wife should leave her husband because he becomes a reclusive, couch-dwelling, buffalo-wing-eating sloth on college football Saturdays. I feel it shows depth, integrity, loyalty, and commitment to stick with the partner you love, even if you don't *like* them every second of your married life. It definitely makes me smile to hear stories of couples who have been married thirty, forty, and fifty years, but life is too short to stay in an unhappy marriage that continues to be miserable despite an effort from both parties involved.

To anyone in an emotionally or physically abusive relationship, believe me when I tell you that you're already *past* the expiration point of the relationship, and you need to get out of there as soon as possible. Marriage is one of the most challenging and rewarding endeavors of the human experience. The rate at which we are learning life lessons combined with the extraordinarily busy lifestyles we live are the two key factors that have raised the divorce rate over the years. I hope this puts a slightly more positive spin on a potentially depressing topic.

If your spouse seems to be a permanent appendage of the couch during every game day, try to cut him some slack and remember why you fell in love with him. And perhaps some buffalo wings are in order, since you washed his lucky jersey.

Do we each have a calling in life or a life purpose? How do I know what mine is?

Yes, we each have a life purpose. As a matter of fact, we each have more than one life purpose. The more advanced you are in terms of wisdom and past life experiences, the more life purposes you'll be able to handle at once. This means you old souls out there (you know who you are) are probably working on a dozen life purposes simultaneously. Why is this? Because you're wise. You're smart, resilient, capable, and can handle more adversity and more challenges in this game of life.

You already know what your life purposes are. Trust me. You know them even if you don't *know* that you know them. What situations and circumstances pop up in your life, day after day, week after week, or year after year? Patterns tend to repeat themselves, and circumstances will also repeat to help you work on lessons that involve your life purposes. If one of your life objectives is to be a leader, then life will continuously hand you people who are followers. It only makes sense. It helps you accomplish what you came here to accomplish. In order to lead, you'll require people who need to be led.

If it's one of your life purposes to be of service to those

in need, you'll inevitably be a magnet for those seeking guidance, mentoring, and healing. It will be your job to provide the world with a bonanza of brotherhood. A cornucopia of compassion. An avalanche of assistance to anyone who crosses your path. And trust me, they *will* cross your path if it's your life purpose to help others. After thinking about it in this way and noticing the reoccurring patterns in your life, do you now have an idea what some of your life purposes are?

I know in the back of your mind, you're thinking, "Aside from leadership and helping others, what are some other life purposes a person can have?" Well, I'm glad you asked. For starters: creativity, forgiveness, humor, being detail-oriented, learning to let go of control, travel, dealing with anger, and staying organized. Then there is teaching, healing, learning to be self-sufficient, overcoming physical hardships, connecting with nature, finding balance, being a mother, and my personal favorite, variety (sampling *everything* life has to offer). This is by no means an exhaustive list. There is so much more. Life purposes are the "why" in the age-old question, "Why are we here?" If you're wondering if self-control is on the list of life purposes, it is. That's why chocolate exists.

Which affects our lives more: free will or destiny?

Once, I gave a psychic reading to a lovely lady named Tonya. After I finished providing her with insight about her love life, I told her I was getting a message about the rear, passenger-side tire on her Chevy Blazer. I warned

Tonya to keep an eye on the tire pressure, because I could see her getting a flat in the near future from driving over broken glass. I had another session with her months later, and she reported to me that two days after our previous reading, the rear, passenger-side tire did go completely flat, causing one heck of an inconvenience for her. Free will does indeed exist. I want to be very clear about this. Most of the time, we are very much in control of our own lives and what we experience. However, there are occasional experiences that were planned into our life chart as something we *must* go through. When this is the case, no amount of planning or being extra cautious will help us avoid the event. Why did Tonya have a flat tire at that point in her life? I don't know. Perhaps, as a lesson in patience. Or, maybe buying a new tire stretched her budget to the max and forced her to work on financial planning. On the other hand, it's possible that she was supposed to meet Mr. Right at the tire shop and wouldn't have had a chance to bump into him unless she had gotten a flat tire. Everything happens for a reason. And whatever the reason, Tonya was destined to get a flat tire at that point in her life. It was unavoidable, despite my previous warning to her.

Once, I told my client, Abby, she needed to be careful to avoid spraining her ankle in the upcoming month of October. Come November, Abby contacted me, saying she tripped going down the stairs, which caused her to get a moderate ankle sprain. She was frustrated that despite her best efforts to be more cautious, it still happened (in

October), when she was most guarded and careful. Again, despite my warning, the accident could not be avoided. Her destiny prevailed over her free will. Perhaps, Abby needed to sprain her ankle at that point in her life to get a few days off work for some much needed rest and relaxation.

Just so you don't get the idea that all of my fate-filled predictions involve injuries and misfortune, let me share an *uplifting* story. I gave a reading to a lady who could be labeled as anything but gullible. Jessica believed what she believed and was a no-nonsense, logically-driven, two-feet-firmly-planted-on-the-ground type of lady. So, when I told her that she would have another child (a girl) who would be born in January of 2013, she didn't believe me. Jessica explained she already had two children and was not trying for a third. Due to major fertility issues and medical complications, doctors told her it was virtually impossible for her to ever conceive another child even if she wanted one. I was unwavering in my prediction, because I felt it was her *fate* to have a third child. One way or another, I believed the little girl was coming into Jessica's life.

A couple of years went by and I bumped into a lady at a Christmas party in late December of 2012. She was Jessica's aunt. She relayed an interesting follow-up story to me. She told me that Jessica *did* get pregnant, unexpectedly, and against all odds. Jessica was pregnant with a girl, just as I'd predicted. She was due to deliver in a couple of weeks (in January 2013), just as I'd told Jessica a few years prior. Although no psychic in the world (including myself) is able to make pin-point accurate predictions, such as this, 100 percent of the time, it always feels good to hit the nail on the head and see a wonderful premonition come to fruition.

Sometimes, flat tires, sprained ankles, and bouncing baby girls are built into our lives as an unavoidable experience we're destined to have. Regarding predictions that are not particularly joyous, my philosophy is this: since none of us have crystal clear knowledge of what our fate has in store for us, we must assume every negative event is changeable. We must be optimistic enough to believe we can make a bad situation better. We must not give up and surrender to fate without a fight. We should not be complacent, assuming fate dictates everything.

In another case, I talked with an older lady who was sweeter than a bagful of sugar. Her name was Sally. I gave her a brief reading in the audience at a large gallery event I was conducting. Sally had been single for quite some time and asked if there was any love life in her future. I told her, "Maybe," and explained it had everything to do with the amount of effort she was willing to put into finding her dream hunk. It had everything to do with Sally's free will. I continued to tell her that *if* she were willing to make an effort and start a relationship with a man, she should pay attention to guys named Donald. I also pictured her potential future mate being an avid walker despite his frequent leg pain, and I could picture him being extremely interested in all aspects of aviation. *If* she ended up with anyone, it would be with this airplane-loving man with a bad leg.

Months passed, and Sally came to see me for a full-length reading. She updated me on her love life. She reported to me she had made an effort to meet someone. His name was not Donald as I predicted, *but* his brother, uncle, and grandfather *are* all named Donald. Sally now takes walks with her new boyfriend as often as possible, and told me he gets along just fine despite complaining his leg bothers him. He *is* passionate about planes and aviation. "In fact," she said, "on our first date, he took me to an airshow. You know, where the planes woo the crowd with fly-bys and aerial tricks."

Sally's face lit up like the Fourth of July, as she told me how everything fell into place as I described it would. I reminded her that she deserves the credit, because she is the one who took destiny by the horns. She threw a lasso around life and pulled happiness into her heart. It was her free will that determined whether or not she'd end up in another relationship, but it was destiny that dictated *who* she would end up with. And apparently, they're a perfect match.

In all of my readings, clients inevitably ask about happiness. They ask me what they can do to find more peace in life, to make their difficult situations easier, and to avoid making mistakes. I encourage each person to use their God-given intuition to navigate their vessel of life. Furthermore, a person must be pro-active, innovative, and forward thinking. We must wield our sword of free will and storm the castle of happiness, plundering and pillaging all the positive experiences life owes us. Happiness is our birthright. So, which has more effect on our lives, fate or free will? I'd say both, equally.

Andy, what do you think is the secret to life?

While a part of me is inclined to get very deep and philosophical here, part of me thinks the answer to this is very simple indeed. First of all, there's not *one* secret to life. The answer is all around us in plain sight.

Stop and enjoy the sunset and sunrise. Allow yourself a mid-afternoon nap, whenever possible. Listen to the stories of a grandparent. Take off your watch, and live in the moment. Allow yourself to cry when you're overly happy and overly sad. Lose yourself from time to time, but don't lose faith. Look forward to tomorrow. Appreciate yesterday. Say a prayer for someone you don't like. Tip your waiters and waitresses well. Nurture something. Say, "I love you," to someone at least once a day. Say, "I love you," to yourself at least once a day. Be silly. Cut yourself a break. Play in the rain. Accept the fact that you don't have all the answers. (Nobody does.) Hold firm to your values, but keep an open mind. Don't judge. Trust yourself, even if you can't trust everyone else. Live as if it were your last day, but have faith that it's not. Count the stars in the sky until you lose track. Smile. Laugh. Breathe.

Chapter 4: Ghosts and Spirits and Angels, Oh My!

What's the difference between an angel and a spirit guide, and how do ghosts fit into all of this?

What a mess we've got here. It seems as though we have a vocabulary train wreck on our hands, so let's try to separate these terms and make sense out of what is what and who is whom. First of all, spirit guides are beings who are assigned to help each one of us through our struggles and our life journey while we're on Earth. You've heard of guardian angels, right? A spirit guide and a guardian angel are one in the same. Just like soda and pop. Same thing, different name.

We each get our own set of spirit guides, and it's their job to make sure we're getting the most out of our experience on this beautiful blue and green planet. Spirit guides are just regular people, like you and me. They are just average Joes who happen to be in-between lifetimes. Spirit guides safely keep an eye on us from Heaven, and sometimes swoop in to literally be by our sides.

Angels are not the same as spirit guides. Angels are more powerful. Unlike spirit guides, angels are not assigned specifically to any one person on Earth. They simply come and go as they please, putting out a fire here, lifting a car off a person there, saving the bicycler from getting hit by the dump truck (and accomplish all of this before lunchtime without breaking a sweat). Angels are messengers from God. Their presence is often known in times of turmoil and distress, but oddly enough, angels seem to disappear as quickly as they mysteriously arrive.

Why is this? Probably because they don't need credit for being the hero. Angels do not have personalities like humans do. They do not feel the need to have their egos stroked, like we humans often do. When an angel appears out of thin air and saves a child from a burning building, they do so out of pure love, not so they can receive a "thank you" from the mayor or get a library named after them.

Now, let's turn our attention to ghosts. Ghosts are human beings who have died, but for numerous reasons, they have not yet crossed over into Heaven. It's not that they're not welcome in Heaven. On the contrary, God is hoping they cross over very soon and would welcome them with streamers, balloons, and a big banner. Why wouldn't a person cross over to the Other Side if it's as beautiful and wondrous as I described earlier? Many reasons. They could be heartbroken and longing to stay with their loved ones on Earth. Perhaps, they didn't finish a project, and they have a sense of unfinished business of which they just can't let go. A dear old dad could decide to hang around in ghost form, frustrated by his own procrastination if he never got around to fixing the house, getting his finances in order, and restoring that 1969 Ford.

Sometimes, a person's religious beliefs play into the decision to "hang around" after passing away. Depending on how a person was raised and what beliefs were engrained in his head, he may fear he'd go to a bad place if he let go and drifted towards the great beyond. I know he would go to Heaven, but in the clouded and confused mind of a ghost, he is afraid. So, in the meantime, he wanders around in an aimless sleepwalking state of existence, too stubborn to cross over into Heaven and too mischievous to refrain from opening your kitchen cabinet or startling the family pet.

Now, we finally come to the term "spirit," which happens to be the wildcard of the vocabulary card deck. It's the variable in the equation. The monkey wrench in our neat set of definitions and terminology. A spirit can refer to a ghost. It can also refer to loved ones in Heaven. The word spirit can describe an ever-loving presence or the essence of God. All of us have heard the term "holy spirit" before. Used in different contexts, it can mean different things.

Do our loved ones in spirit form still come around us and take an interest in what we're doing here?

Let me flip this question back around on you. Would you still take an interest in your family and what they're doing on Earth, once you've crossed over into Heaven? Of course you would! Yes, our loved ones in Heaven can and *do* come around us. In fact, they visit us often. They know what shenanigans we're getting into, and they view us like we're their favorite reality show. Allow me to share a few stories, proving just how much our loved ones in spirit form know about our daily lives.

Her name was Melissa. She was a daughter, sister, cousin, and friend to those she left behind. Melissa was a young lady who died a few years prior, and several of her family members came to my office in hope that she would come through with some messages. And come through she did! Melissa was one of the strongest and most direct spirits who has ever contacted me, and our communication lines were definitely clear. It turned into a rapid-fire session of validating messages for each of the ten individuals present at my office.

Melissa wanted me to tell her sister, Ellie, "You're being a cheapskate by using *my* eye shadow. Go out and buy your own!" Ellie agreed, and informed me her sister Melissa was known for her eye shadow, wearing dozens and dozens of colors from week to week. Ellie admitted to using Melissa's eye shadow since her death and seemed astonished to hear that Melissa actually knew about this.

Melissa wanted me to shift over to her cousin, Craig, and she said he would be going to Colorado soon. Craig became bug-eyed, as he validated this was true. The very next week, he was supposed to be going on a road trip to the Rocky Mountains. Melissa couldn't resist getting in a quick, loving jab at her cousin Craig, as she asked me to give him a hard time about being a mediocre skier. Craig sheepishly chuckled and admitted he had some skiing injuries and mishaps in the past, and Melissa knew about it when she was alive. While skiing in Colorado, he knew Melissa would be there in spirit, laughing every time he fell.

Melissa then wanted me to talk with her other cousin, Garrett, who was present in the room. Garrett looked to be around 17 years old. He appeared very nervous, as he anticipated what Melissa might know about his actions since her death. First of all, she wanted me to tell Garrett that his new girlfriend was a "dingbat." The entire family, including Garrett, laughed at this comment coming from Melissa, and they all agreed the statement was accurate. Although obligated to be nice to her for Garrett's sake, the family unanimously felt his girlfriend lacked common sense, to say the least. Then, Melissa wanted me to warn him that he should not drive when he is angry, because he'll tend to speed and get speeding tickets. Garrett held his breath and turned three different shades of pink.

His mom, who was in the room, practically stared a hole through him. Voice trembling, Garrett confessed to what Melissa said from beyond the grave. He admitted to his mom and the rest of the family for the first time that the previous night he was out driving, attempting to clear his mind while he was angry, and he did in fact get a speeding ticket. The message from Melissa proved to the whole family she not only takes an active interest in their lives, but she was probably riding shotgun with Garrett the previous night, as he got pulled over for speeding. Talk about instant validation! Melissa just knocked their socks off.

Melissa had one final message, a warning. She said, "I'll be turning lights on and off as a sign that I'm still alive and with the family in spirit." We concluded the hour-long family reading, and Melissa's speed demon of a cousin went around the corner to use the restroom (and probably to hide from his mother, who was still angry about the speeding ticket). Garrett quickly returned just a few seconds later, with tears in his eyes. He appeared very shaken and upset, and the family asked him what on Earth was the matter. Trying to stay composed, he muttered, "I was just in the bathroom peeing, and the lights suddenly went out." Garrett's tears were not those of fear or sadness, but of joy. I went to inspect the bathroom light, and discovered it was not burnt out, but had been *unscrewed!* With a stern twist, I tightened the light bulb, and it came back on. I chuckled to myself, and wanted to give Melissa a standing ovation.

Later that night, I said a prayer of gratitude and thanked Melissa for coming through so strongly. I couldn't thank her enough for providing validation to her family that she's still alive in Heaven and knows what's going on in their lives.

When spirits visit us from Heaven, they don't always interfere with our light bulbs and electronics, but sometimes they take an interest in our finances. While reading a young man named Josh who was a little bit skeptical, I made a connection with his grandpa who passed away. His grandpa wanted me to give Josh a hard time for not knowing how to correctly make out a personal check. Hoping and praying this message would be well received, I reluctantly delivered the message from grandpa to Josh. Luckily, Josh smiled, and said just two days prior, he attempted to fill out a personal check only to make an error *three* times in a row. After three voided checks, I'm sure Josh's grandpa was having a good laugh. Although the checkbook incident wasn't a life-changing or exciting moment in Josh's life, grandpa's comment proved that he takes an interest in Josh's day-to-day activities and knows what's happening.

I once connected to a lady named Lanesha in the audience at one of my shows and felt the presence of her dad who passed away a few years earlier. He kept asking me to talk to Lanesha about "condensing the accounts," and how it was such a good idea. I asked Lanesha if she knew what her dad was talking about. She knew what he was referring to and said that in recent months, she was getting rid of several bank accounts that she no longer needed and was condensing all of her money into just two accounts that she more closely monitored.

Lanesha explained that when her father was alive, he was very organized when it came to finances. He was the go-to person for anyone in the family who had questions about money. Our loved ones on the Other Side know everything we're doing! They know when we've voided checks, and they know when we've condensed our accounts.

Your family members and friends in Heaven still keep

tabs on what you're currently doing. This is proven to me repeatedly, week in and week out in medium sessions, as I relay information from spirits. When they're not talking about our bank accounts and speeding tickets, they're talking about vacations. Like the time I was meeting with Ashley and her deceased sister came through wanting me to bring up Ashley's recent trip to Disney World. Ashley then informed me that she and her family just returned from "the happiest place on Earth" the previous week.

Then there's the time Karen's deceased husband wanted me to ask her if she was all packed and ready for New York. Karen validated that she was leaving for the Big Apple the very next morning. She looked astonished. I told Karen she really shouldn't be so surprised, and her husband would be going with her on this trip. I lightened the mood by joking he would be packing lightly now that he's in spirit form. She smiled and laughed, and felt comforted knowing that her husband is doing fantastic in Heaven. In another reading, Stephanie's deceased father wanted me to mention Stephanie going to South Dakota, and how this was a common occurrence. With teary eyes, Stephanie said South Dakota was their family's favorite place to visit, and her dad always insisted they go there for vacation. She had, in fact, travelled to South Dakota a half-dozen times in recent years since his passing.

To hammer home the point that deceased loved ones are up-to-date with our current events, I'll leave you with a heart-warming story about sidewalk chalk. My client was a young lady named Amanda, who unfortunately had lost her husband. He was in the military, and after a serious injury in Afghanistan, he returned home and passed away a year later due to complications from the initial wound. Amanda was the youngest widow I've ever read. She was strong and proud and had a big heart. She told me she started a non-profit organization in memory of her husband. On top of all this, Amanda still had enough energy to be a wonderful mother. She was left to raise two young girls on her own.

We received several validating messages from her late husband. He seemed to be well-informed about their kids, Amanda's eating habits, finances, and even some inside jokes they shared when he was alive. One of the last messages he gave had to do with their seven-year-old daughter, Emma. He said to me, "When Emma is using sidewalk chalk to color on the driveway, she needs to choose a new piece of chalk when one starts to get worn down. Otherwise, she'll end up accidentally scraping her knuckles on the sidewalk." Amanda got very choked up after hearing this message from her husband.

She explained why it made so much sense. Amanda said, "Just a few weeks earlier, Emma was coloring in the driveway with sidewalk chalk." At this point, Amanda's voice was shaking, as she attempted to keep it together. She explained that Emma was writing a letter on the driveway for her daddy in Heaven. When she got to the end of the letter and went to sign her name, the chalk was worn down to a nub. Instead of signing "Emma," she was only able to write "Em" before the chalk was too small to use.

I felt a lump in my throat when I heard this, and I unexpectedly found *myself* fighting back tears. I said, "Well, I bet she nearly scraped her fingers on the cement trying to finish that letter to her dad, didn't she?"

Emma's dad was there. He read her letter. In fact, I can just picture him sitting right next to her on the driveway in spirit form, watching her and thinking to himself how much she looks like her mother.

Whether you're coloring, going on a trip, driving too fast, or voiding a check, your loved ones are with you. They see you. They hear you. Every time you miss them and wonder if they're around, please breathe easily knowing they are present. Every now and then, when you're thinking about them and are lucky enough to feel their presence or smell their scent, know they are giving you a big spiritual bear hug from the Other Side. Remember, you are their favorite reality show. And they have the best seat in the house to watch you.

Can ghosts hurt us or harm us physically?

No, I don't believe they can. I know some people would disagree with me on this subject. If you've watched any one of the infinite number of ghost shows on television recently, you've probably noticed they portray ghosts as snarling beasts. Savage demonic entities who are out for blood. In many cases, people claim to have been scratched, hit, and even pushed down a flight of stairs by unseen, evil forces.

When there is a combative or rambunctious ghost who has the potential to bring us harm, our spirit guides and even angels will intervene to protect us. Spirit guides, angels, and any of your loved ones in Heaven are much more powerful than a confused, cranky ghost. Therefore, a ghost could not cause physical harm to a person.

On the other hand, a ghost can act as an emotional vampire, sucking the positive energy right out of you quicker than bathwater going down the drain. They can gain strength from your negative thoughts and your fear. The most that ghosts can do is scare us, drain us, or put us in a bad mood (but only if we let them). If you ever feel an unseen "somebody" following right behind you as you walk up the basement stairs, turn around and tell them to back off. If you ever experience a heavy feeling in the room with you, say out loud, "I am more powerful than you and want to be left alone. This is my space. Go away. Go towards the light." Rest assured, my ghost-hunting friends, you cannot be physically hurt by things that go bump in the night, and as long as you call on angels or your spirit guides for protection, you reduce the risk of even being *emotionally* harmed by a ghost.

How do I know who my spirit guide is?

I get asked this question on a daily basis, and most people are surprised to hear they don't have just one spirit guide. We have more than one of these spiritual guidance counselors. We all have at least two of them because even the seemingly simplest person is still complicated enough to need more than one helper. So how do you know who they are? At the risk of sounding cheeky, my semi-sarcastic and honest answer is, "Ask them."

The most intelligent people in the world are those who ask the most questions. If you want answers, if you want enlightenment, if you want the key to the lockbox of mystery, or even to establish a personal relationship with your spirit guides, then ask questions. Tonight, as you lie in bed and think about life, say a silent, inquisitive prayer requesting the names and job duties of your spirit guides. If, after asking their names, nothing comes to you and their names don't pop into your noggin, be patient, and try again tomorrow.

If you continuously fail to make contact with your spirit guides, you may want to try a different mode of communication to discover their identity. After all, not all spirit guides are auditory in the way they make their presence known. If you're more of a visual person, keep your eyes peeled for a sign in your physical surroundings. If you're a vivid dreamer, your spirit guides may try to introduce themselves to you in a dream while you're sound asleep.

Learning who your spirit guides are and communicating with them is not something that can be forced. It must come naturally. If, on the other hand, the name of your spirit guide *does* suddenly and unexpectedly fire through the synapses of your brain, trust it. Go with it. Even if the name doesn't seem familiar. After all, 95% of the time, our spirit guides are *not* deceased family members. Spirit guides come from all corners of the globe, and sometimes have foreign or unfamiliar names.

A long time ago, while attempting to identify my guides, I wasn't expecting the name of one of my guides to be Henry. But it was. Years later, I wasn't expecting another spirit guide to reveal herself as Jasmine. But she did.

Spirit guides can be surprisingly inventive and creative when it comes to getting our attention. One time while sitting in my office, waiting for my client to arrive, I asked the universe, "Who is the main spirit guide of the client I'm about to meet?" Although "hearing" nothing, I happened to look at the bottom portion of the couch right in front of me and noticed some individual dog hairs clinging to the couch. The hairs seemed to be aligned in the strangest formation. I got out of my chair and bent over for a closer inspection. Individual dog hairs (from my dog Zico) had stuck to the couch in a way that perfectly spelled out the word, "Max." I know what you're thinking. No, this wasn't like those people who swear to see the Virgin Mary in their grilled cheese sandwich or find a potato chip in the formation of Abraham Lincoln and promptly ask $1,000 for it on an Internet auction site. The hairs on my couch spelled out the name, "Max," as clear as day, and I noticed it at the exact moment I asked for the name of my client's spirit guide.

My client obviously had spirit guides who were more comfortable communicating through visual means. Did

I tell my client I received the information through the arrangement of dog hairs on my couch? Nope. People think psychics are weird enough as it is. If word gets out that my couch gives me psychic messages, I may be trading in my psychic badge for a big, white, straightjacket. I did, however, explain to my client with a smile on my face that her spirit guide Max would be using visual means to communicate with her in the future. She said it made sense to her, because she is a very visual person by nature and is always on the lookout for signs and messages in her physical surroundings. Furthermore, she said she has always had a fondness for the name Max and never really knew why. Now, she knows.

Sometimes, my clients come to me specifically hoping to be introduced to their spirit guides. Enthusiastically, I oblige since it's one of my favorite subjects to discuss with them. Would you be surprised if I said you *already* know who your spirit guides are? It's true. You already know them because you personally selected them before coming into this lifetime. We all select our own spirit guides before we are born. We do this while planning our lives on the Other Side.

We don't remember planning our lifetime and selecting our own spirit guides, because most of the time in our day-to-day lives, we operate using our conscious minds. However, it's the *subconscious* mind and our higher-selves that store all the information, such as, who your spirit guides are, why you are here, and what Heaven is like. Occasionally, I'll meet with a client who has what I call "spirit memory," which simply means they're somehow able to tap into their subconscious more easily. Therefore, when I give them the names of their spirit guides, it rings true. It seems familiar to them. A part of their soul still remembers selecting their particular group of guardian angels.

Those with good spirit memory will often have a natural love for the name even before they discover it's the name of their spirit guide. When this happens, they'll often say, "Wow, that's what I almost named my first born child," or "Holy cow, that's what I named my car," or, "That's what I just named my puppy!"

We all know our spirit guides even if we don't *know* that we know them. When we have a conscious recollection of our spirit guides' names, they often become our favorite names. Maybe it's because our spirit guides are truly our best friends.

Do our spirit guides protect us?

Yes, they protect us when it's in everyone's best interest to do so. Of course, keep in mind they will not always baby us and make life perfectly easy for us. Doing so would deprive us of the chance to overcome hardship and adversity in our crazy existence here on Earth, which we now know is vital in our effort to acquire wisdom. However, if your spirit guides notice you're running the risk of getting into a car accident, and it's not written into your life plan to experience this, they will do whatever they can to help avert this calamity. If it was never written in the stars for your son to break his leg in today's football game, his spirit guides can cause the coach to pull him out of the game just before this would happen. If, after a frustrating day at work, you simply don't have the energy or patience to deal with the jerk at checkout lane number four at the grocery store, your spirit guides will subconsciously steer you towards checkout lane eight to avoid him. They protect you in ways too numerous to count, but usually their influence is so subtle we don't realize when it happens.

Do angels have wings?

I'm not sure. I've never seen a winged one myself. Why *couldn't* angels have wings? Perhaps, they do. Maybe they can fly, and maybe they can't. My intuition is silent on the matter. I do know wings symbolize power, grace, and freedom, which are traits angels definitely possess. In any case, I believe angels are real.

One time, I volunteered as a bell-ringer for the Salvation Army right before the holidays. It was frigid outside. I could no longer feel my fingers or toes, and the pins-and-needles feeling coursed through my bloodstream. The bone-chilling wind blew relentlessly. Not wanting to leave my station and fearing this could turn into a slight case of very real frostbite, I said a silent prayer asking for some help or relief. Or more importantly, warmth!

Two minutes later, a lady came out of the grocery store where I was standing, and she handed me a package of hand and foot warmers. You know, the kind you tuck inside your gloves and shoes, and they are chemically activated to warm up the extremities. She was my angel that night. Whoever she was. Sometimes, I still think of her and am grateful the little pinkies on my hands and feet are still in working order because of the warmth she provided.

There is also an angel living in my house. I see him every day. Sometimes his breath doesn't smell too good, and he sheds like crazy. Even licks his own butt from time to time. Zico is my angel. He is my best friend. He is my protector, my Godsend, my loyal, unwavering, and constant companion. Zico goes *everywhere* with me. Even to work, where he divides his time evenly between guard dog of the front door, and therapy dog in my reading room. Do angels have wings? Zico doesn't. But then again, neither did the lady who allowed me to warm my hands and feet outside the grocery store that winter night.

I was once in a session with a sweet, older lady named Betty, who appeared to be in her seventies. She had lived a hard life and was a serious lady who was not prone to flights of fancy. If Betty had something to say, by gosh, you listened. And listen I did, as she relayed a jaw-dropping story about an angel.

Betty explained that one time, she walked into her bedroom and gasped as she laid eyes on a seven-foot-tall winged angel standing in the corner of her dimly lit bedroom. She said she whipped around to flip the light on, and by the time she turned again to face the angelic being, it had vanished. The next day, she was vacuuming her bedroom floor and noticed a large, grayish-white feather in the same corner of her room she had previously seen the angel. Betty assured me she doesn't own any pillows or bed comforters containing feathers. She doubted a random feather could have accidentally drifted into that corner of her bedroom, because it was tucked away in a little nook where nobody walked or went near.

Does Betty have in her possession physical evidence that angels are real? I'd like to think she does. Apparently, some angels really do have wings, and one was kind enough to leave Betty a little souvenir. As I type these words and look over at Zico, who is curled up and sleeping like an angel on the floor, I can't help but think to myself that angels come in all shapes and sizes. Some have wings, and some have brown fur.

Are ghosts to blame for all the weird occurrences around the house?

Not necessarily. First, blame the cat. I'm not saying this because I dislike cats. I'm saying this because they're mischievous. Any kind of trouble they *can* cause, they *will* cause. If the cat is innocent, then blame the youngest child in the household for the strange occurrences. Why the *youngest* child? Because the older child used to make the mistake of getting caught, but now he has the wisdom and verbal skills to coerce the younger sibling into doing his dirty work. If the younger child has played no part in weird phenomena happening in the home, then it's possible it was a ghost.

However, ghosts are much rarer than you would think.

The dozens of ghost hunting shows on television have brainwashed us into thinking there are ghosts around every corner, in every dark hallway, lurking in the shadows. But it's usually not the case.

Many of the odd occurrences around your home can be attributed to your own energy. The electromagnetic energy field around your body is very volatile and prone to flaring outwards just like the coronal mass ejections our sun spews out from time to time. Your electromagnetic field is finicky and has unpredictable bursts. When this happens, it's usually due to our intense emotions. Anger, frustration, anticipation, extreme empathy, or nervousness. All of these can drastically affect our energy fields when we experience them in large and intense doses.

When our energy fields flare out in all directions, they can interfere with electronics and physical objects around our home. Our radios may change stations all on their own. Our DVD players may turn themselves on even though we're not near the remote control. Our laptop computers will freeze or turn themselves off even though they are fully charged. When our emotional and psychic energies interfere with things around our homes, objects can move, fall, and be rearranged without you even touching them.

I've personally seen it happen too many times to count and have heard dozens of stories from others who have experienced this phenomenon. I once saw a small piece of paper directly in front of me slide six inches across the desk, as if someone deliberately moved it. There was no draft in the room. I was not scared because I knew it wasn't a ghost. It was my own energy inadvertently moving the piece of paper. I knew this because I was journaling on the computer at the time of the incident and experiencing intense emotions. Even if it was a ghost, I still would not have been frightened. Ghosts cannot hurt you, me, or anyone else, as we discussed earlier.

So, the next time you see a rocking chair swing back and forth on its own accord, the television scrolling through channels by itself, or your gaming system turning on by the hand of an unseen force, stop and pay attention to the mood you are in. If you're emotionally charged at that moment, then you're most likely causing the strange occurrence yourself and are ghost-free (as long as you can account for your youngest born child and the family cat).

Can my spirit guides and those of my loved ones communicate with one another?

You betcha. They communicate with each other fairly frequently. Imagine all of your spirit guides and the spirit guides of your loved ones getting together to huddle and strategize, just like a football team. Communication is of the utmost importance, not only between ourselves, but also for our guardian angels. Since everything we do affects everything in the lives of our loved ones, it's a game of cause and effect, like a line of dominos toppling over. Our lives are a cosmic pinball machine of actions and reactions that need to fit together in just the right way. Our spirit guides make sure everything is going according to plan and they make alterations in our life charts as needed.

Your own personal spirit guides have *your* best interests in mind, and the spirit guides of your loved ones have *their* best interests in mind. However, since we are all so closely connected, it becomes rather complicated to make sure *everyone* is on track and experiencing what they came here to experience. Our spirit guides have their work cut out for them. Lucky for us, they are more than qualified to manage the complicated life chart we have planned for ourselves. After all, our spirit guides helped us plan this crazy journey before we got here, so they know what's coming our way long before it happens.

Why is it that ghosts are more likely to hang around in old houses and historical places?

The longer a place has existed, the more activities have taken place there. An old house or place of historical interest has had a lot of traffic through it. Many events have taken place on the property. With such a rich history, it raises the odds that someone may have died on that property, therefore, making it a possibility that a ghost might be roaming around the location.

Additionally, places of historical interest are often the sites in which some conflict took place. Whether it was a war, a struggle, a battle for resources, or a different type of skirmish, death may have unfortunately been involved. When people die in a dramatic or violent fashion, such as in battle, this raises the likelihood they could be hanging around in ghost form. Traumatic deaths are so jarring, shocking, and unexpected that they leave a person confused. A ghost wandering around the Gettysburg Battlefield may not even know he died in the Civil War, because he is in a muddled, dream-like state of existence. He'll eventually cross over to Heaven, but only when he's good and ready (and has had the pleasure of spooking plenty of ghost hunters and tourists, of course).

One other angle to consider is that sometimes ghost hauntings are confused with imprints, which is a term used to describe the leftover energy and emotions hanging around a particular place. A house is the location for countless birthday parties, arguments, family reunions, laughter, injuries, births, deaths, rearranging, love making, renovating, and the full spectrum of human behaviors over several decades. The property builds up quite an imprint of energy and emotions. The feelings that spill out from each and every person in a location do not simply disappear. The emotions hang around, thick in the air, like Florida humidity in the summer. Imprints can be good, bad, or indifferent. Since imprints have such a strong impact on us, we often mislabel a place as haunted when it has simply been stamped with emotions and energy throughout the years.

Are children better at perceiving the presence of ghosts and angels?

Children *are* the most psychic beings on the planet. It's true. They perceive ghosts, angels, spirit guides, and deceased loved ones as clearly and vividly as they can see you standing in front of them. There are many reasons for this.

First of all, a child's head is not filled with the useless information we adults deem so important. As adults, our memory banks are filled with an endless array of facts and information. The color of the dress you wore to your junior year prom. The amount of fat grams in a chocolate ice cream sandwich. The fastest route from downtown to your front door. How much money is in which account, and what bills are due at what time. It's unfathomable how much information is stored right between our ears, in the back corners and cellars of our minds.

Kids' brains aren't saturated with all this information, yet, and they're able to access different and unique areas of their brains which allow them to perceive the world differently. They are accessing more areas of the brain linked to creativity, language, emotion, impulsivity, and empathy, which are the chambers that store intuition. Over the years, adults have become more accustomed to accessing parts of their brain involving logic, rational thinking, problem solving, mathematics, and factual information. These are the parts of our brains that hinder psychic abilities and prevent access to our intuition.

Another reason children are highly intuitive is because they have freshly arrived here from the Other Side. A three-year-old girl is only three years removed from Heaven. Three years removed from her true self, unlimited potential, and functioning at a higher vibration.

We are all at our psychic peaks while on the Other Side. All the answers are clear to us. All the wisdom is in our back pockets. We are truly limitless in what we can do, sense, and achieve when we are in Heaven. Some of this sticks with children when they are young, until they begin to be affected by the world around them and forget who they are and why they're here. How then do some people manage to hold onto their intuition as they grow up? It's by refusing to forget where they came from.

As adults, most of us have been told not to believe in nonsense and fairy tales. We feel if we admit to seeing ghosts and other things that "don't exist," we *could* be labeled as nutcases and looked down on by the more rational people in our lives. Since seeing unexplained entities is still taboo in many circles of society, many adults don't talk about it much and dismiss it when it actually happens.

A young boy, on the other hand, may not have been told that ghosts, angels, and spirit guides don't exist. He has yet to be trained not to talk about these experiences. Therefore, when he does see a ghost, angel, spirit guide, or your dead grandfather, he reports the experience in an innocent and matter-of-fact way. To him, it's simply an observation, and the young boy has no reason to second guess what he experienced.

The worst thing parents can do is to make their children feel guilty or ashamed for seeing something with their intuitive senses. It frustrates me when a mom doesn't take her child's reports of seeing ghosts or deceased loved ones seriously. Parents' insecurities about the paranormal are no good reason for making their child feel ashamed or embarrassed for having intuitive abilities. A skeptical or overprotective parent needs to keep in mind that just because something cannot be fully explained doesn't mean it's bad, evil, or harmful.

Parents who are not educated about psychic phenomena tend to fear the unknown and attribute their child's experiences to "trickery of the devil." This fear-based approach is not helpful for a child. Fear breeds more fear. And usually, a child will not be afraid of something unless he's been *taught* to fear it. The best thing a parent of an intuitive child can do is remain open-minded, tell the child there's nothing to be afraid of, and ask more open-ended questions. "Tell me about what you saw," or "How did it make you feel?" is a heck of a lot more helpful than telling a child, "You didn't see anything," or "It was just your imagination."

Since spirit guides are just regular people, do they have unique personalities like us?

Yes. Just as Mother Earth is home to a plethora of personalities, Heaven is also filled with its fair share of characters, including spirit guides. Many spirit guides are funny. In fact, downright hilarious! I guess when we're not bogged down by the seriousness of work, finances, and physical hardships, all of us are funny at the core. Our spirit guides in Heaven are just regular people like you and me. In Heaven, they don't have the struggles we have, and are prone to tapping into their well of humor more often.

Then again, once in a great while, I will sense that my client has a spirit guide who is as dry as an overcooked burger. You know the kind I'm talking about. Stoic. Serious. An unflinching face that doesn't change regardless of their mood. Yes, some spirit guides fail to let their inner jokester out. They may not win the Miss Congeniality award or woo you with their charisma, but by gosh, they'll help keep you organized with their no-nonsense demeanor. The world needs guardian angels like these. They keep us care-free and unorganized individuals in line and out of trouble.

Some spirit guides use curse words. Honestly. I'm often like a parrot in my psychic readings, simply repeating what I'm hearing from my client's spirit guides. However, when my client's spirit guides choose to express themselves with language as dirty as a used Kleenex, I'd rather paraphrase and deliver the cleaner, edited version to my client. Unique personalities? Yep, spirit guides have got 'em.

Spirit guides also have their own, unique sense of fashion. They often give me mental images of their appearance. Sometimes, spirit guides dress in three-piece, pinstriped suits that would impress a fashion expert from New York or Paris. Some spirit guides wear dresses. Others wear jeans and a t-shirt. Whether they look polished and presentable or appear as if they washed up on shore from a shipwreck, spirit guides are inclined to express themselves through their sense of fashion.

One of my wife's spirit guides, Mirinu, actually has the audacity to go shirtless and flaunt his muscles. He appeared to me in this fashion when I assisted Kenzie in identifying all five of her guardian angels. I set my ego aside, and unenthusiastically explained to her that Mirinu has the chiseled muscles of an Olympic gymnast. I don't know if he's trying to "one up" me with his bronzed skin and toned physique, but I'd like to give him a piece of my mind. Then again, if I start arguing with invisible beings, I'm afraid I'll soon be contacted by the nearest licensed mental health practitioner and given a lengthy evaluation.

Since there's no dress code in Heaven, I've decided when I get back there, I'm wearing nothing but my soccer ball pajama pants and an old t-shirt that's been washed so many times it's softer than silk. Why not? God's not judging me, and besides, He knows I love soccer and being comfortable. What would you wear for the rest of eternity? Your bathrobe? Your fuzzy, pink slippers? Your oversized sweatshirt from college? Nothing at all? Shame on you! Then again, if you walked around Heaven in your birthday suit, you may draw a bigger following than Jesus Christ himself. Who knows?

Some spirit guides have tattoos. If you find it hard to believe that one of your spirit guides may have "Mom" tattooed on his chest, let me explain. Spirit guides tend to look like a middle-aged version of how they appeared in their most recent past lifetime. Therefore, if they had tattoos when they were alive, they are probably still sporting them.

Since they have unique personalities just like you and me, they have likes, dislikes, preferences, opinions, and a history all their own. Many times, you'll actually have a lot in common with your spirit guides. If they loved to garden, they'll be with you when you're weeding the flowerbed. If they loved to bake in their past lifetimes, you'll probably feel their presence in the kitchen when you lick the beaters after whipping up a cake. Wasn't that the best part of helping someone bake when you were young? Licking the beaters! One of the best little pleasures of life, if you ask me.

Is there any proof spirit guides are real?

At the beginning of this book, I promised to tell you a story about a guardian angel named Lefty. I'm a man of my word. So here it goes. I was meditating prior to a reading, just like I always do, and I felt the presence of a spirit guide come to me. Since spirit guides don't get stuck in rush hour traffic, it's not unusual for them to "arrive" prior to my client. They'll tell me interesting information about the client I'm going to meet.

I could sense this particular spirit guide was a male. Through the little inner voice of my intuition, I could hear him tell me that his name was Lefty. I thought to myself, "What an unusual name."

As I pondered if this might be a nickname, he said very directly, "My name is Ken 'Lefty' Douglas."

My ears (or rather, my intuition) perked up. He had my attention. I concentrated as this invisible presence described to me everything about his past lifetime. "I was rather tall," he said. "Over six feet tall. I played AA baseball on the West Coast in the early 1900s. I was a left-handed pitcher, which is why they called me 'Lefty.' I currently help your client with her organizational skills and her attention to detail."

"Holy shish kebabs," I thought to myself. "This is weird." Nevertheless, I relayed all the information about Lefty to my client. She felt comforted knowing she had a guardian angel helping her with her attention to detail. Later that night, I had a few friends over to my house. One of them asked me if I had given any interesting readings recently.

"I guess," I answered. "I gave a reading to a lady today. She apparently has a spirit guide named Lefty Douglas who says he played semi-pro baseball on the West Coast or something."

My friend lit up with excitement and suggested we research this character online to verify his existence through baseball records. I whole-heartedly believe the information I share during readings is accurate, but in that moment, I brushed off my friend, suggesting we wouldn't find any information online about the old baseball player. I politely changed the subject.

Later that night, I couldn't sleep. Eventually, I rolled out of bed and wandered to my computer. I scrolled through century-old baseball statistics, attempting to find information on a guy named Ken "Lefty" Douglas. My searches continuously came up empty. As I was about to give up, something at the very bottom of the search engine caught my attention. It appeared to be what I was looking for. Bingo! I clicked on the link and held my breath.

The display contained baseball rosters and statistics

from the early 1900s. It showed a man named Ken "Lefty" Douglas was born in 1901. I read that he played semi-pro baseball for AA teams on the West Coast, including San Francisco, Portland, and Los Angeles. The left-handed pitcher stood 6'2". Every single piece of information this spirit guide told me about himself prior to the reading with my client was entirely and completely accurate. He really existed!

My research showed Ken "Lefty" Douglas passed away in Sacramento, California, at age 67. Since then, he has taken on the responsibility of becoming a spirit guide, helping my client stay organized and detail-oriented. Staring at my computer screen on that sleepless night is something I'll never forget. It gave me goose bumps and made me teary-eyed. I felt validated. For me, it was proof positive that guardian angels are real beings. They are not figments of our imagination that we concoct in order to give ourselves peace of mind. They are not imaginary friends. They are real. They have lived on this Earth before. Spirit guides are now in Heaven and come to help us in our times of need. If you're looking for something to believe in; perhaps, this is it. I have always believed in guardian angels. An old baseball player named "Lefty" is all the proof I need to keep on believing this.

Do we have the same spirit guides in this lifetime as we had in previous lifetimes?

As I mentioned earlier, I attended a small Catholic school from kindergarten until eighth grade. My second grade teacher was a nun. Her name was Sister Georgia Jean. I referred to her as "Mean Georgia Jean," although this pet name for her stayed safely inside my little second-grade brain, lest she find out and send me home with yet another disciplinary note.

She made my life miserable for an entire school year. I was an opinionated and free spirited walking target for her disciplinary arrow. And her relentless arrow of order never missed its mark. Several times, I went home with my head down in shame because I had to report to my mom that I got in trouble (again). In Sister Georgia Jean's defense though, I'm sure she wasn't all bad.

As an adult, I no longer have the urge to call her "Mean" Georgia Jean. I'm sure she meant well, and I believe that underneath her pursed lips and furrowed eyebrows, she had my best interests in mind. Nevertheless, the most amazing day of my second-grade school year was the *last* day of my second-grade school year. The sweet release of summer ushered in a new chapter in my life. A fresh start. And the next year I would be learning brand-new lessons with a brand-new teacher.

This is similar to how our spirit guides change, as we incarnate from one lifetime to another. We all live more than one lifetime. I want you to think of each lifetime as a new grade level in school. As we make our way through school, we learn different lessons from grade to grade and we typically get new teachers each year. Similarly, as we evolve from lifetime to lifetime, we often get new spirit guides each incarnation. Why is this? Because, just as in school, the lessons change from one lifetime to the next, and we require new instructors who specialize in teaching us what we need to learn at the time.

Sometimes, we'll have a spirit guide who has helped us in past incarnations, but we're often given a new batch of spirit guides when we enter into another incarnation on Earth. If you make it to Heaven before I do, look up Sister Georgia Jean and jokingly tell her that I have a bone to pick with her. And while you're at it, give her a hug from me for being a dedicated and passionate teacher for so many years. Lord knows how underappreciated teachers are.

Andy, what kind of spirit guides do you have?

The best kind. For a long time I've known I have a spirit guide named Henry. He has dark brown hair, stands at an average height, has a square jaw, and a stocky build. Henry helps me with organization, memory, and keeping my ducks in a row. Thanks to Henry, my ducks stay in line rather than scattering like third graders at recess. He helps me with intellectual matters and provides me with logical reasoning skills in times of mayhem. Apparently, Henry is also fairly protective of me and rather nosy at times. One of my mentors, Patty, occasionally does some energy work on me, taking away fatigue and aligning my body, mind, and spirit. She often asks Henry to step back and leave me alone for a minute so she can conduct her energy work. I guess spirit guides can be like over-protective parents at times, finding it difficult to let go of our hands and trust that we'll be okay out in the real world without them at our sides.

Jasmine is a relatively new discovery for me. She suddenly barged through my spiritual doorway and announced her presence when I first began my intuitive work. Jasmine is the spirit guide who helps me with intuition and emotions. She monitors areas of my life related to compassion, empathy, and relationships. She's typically present during my psychic readings, acting as the bridge that connects me to my higher self. Her gentle touch keeps me grounded when I'm frazzled. I like to think of her as my spiritual blood pressure medication. Viewing her in this light, my insurance company should write her a thank you letter for keeping me healthy and mentally stable.

I am one of the minorities who is lucky enough to have a deceased loved one in my repertoire of spirit guides. My Grandma Myers died in 2008. I personally and intuitively feel her as one of my guardian angels, and several other reputable, intuitive individuals have independently corroborated the fact that my Grandma Myers is officially my third spirit guide. What does she help with? Humor. Curiosity. Adventure. Helping me not to take life too seriously, and reminding me to cut myself a break from time to time. I can feel her encouraging my creative side just as she did when she was alive. I feel her riding shotgun next to me as I look out my car window at a beautiful sunset. She loved life and passed on her zest for adventure to me. With her as my North Star, my guiding light on my journey through life, I feel confident I'll stay on course.

I have a fourth spirit guide as well. It's a female. Not sure of her name or what she does for me. Why? Because she's not with me at this point in time. Yep. Hasn't shown up. Not yet reported for duty. Is she lazy? Did she oversleep? Does she have too much faith that I can handle the craziness life throws at me? I don't know. I *do* know that occasionally, particular spirit guides will be absent for many years, and then will suddenly swoop into our lives and help with certain challenges that correlate to their area of expertise.

It's not uncommon for us to have a spirit guide who hasn't yet arrived. Sometimes, a spirit guide will patiently wait until we stumble upon a particular chapter of our lives in which they are assigned to help. Although one of my female spirit guides is not active in my life, I know she'll show up when the time is right. How do I know she exists? It's like I see a conference room table where a name card is placed in front of each seat, indicating who is expected to be present at the meeting. Henry, Jasmine, and my Grandma Myers have all taken their seats at the table of my life. One seat remains empty, reserved for the fashionably late spirit guide whom I'll graciously rely on at some point in the future. I hope she's a good one. I'll take all the help I can get!

Chapter 5: Intuition and Receiving Psychic Messages

Does accessing our intuition make us more susceptible to bad energies?

It depends on your definition of "bad energies." I don't believe opening up your psychic senses makes you vulnerable to goblins and demonic presences. Ghouls, demonic entities, and the devil himself are not real. Although many people will disagree, I'm holding true to my belief on this matter. They are not real.

I've never once in my life had a traumatic experience while remaining intuitively open because I don't *want* to. I do not invite dark presences into my life. I don't believe in the devil, and I know that ghosts cannot hurt me. I'm too busy "staying in the light" to be afraid of the unknown. Regarding demonic presences: they cannot get me because they are not real. If they are real, they cannot find me. And even if they are real and find me, God and my guardian angels would never let them harm me. Or you. Trust me, you are protected. The worst we may ever have to deal with is Bigfoot, and if you throw some beef jerky in his general direction to distract him, I have faith *he* won't harm you, either.

On the other hand, being open-minded and intuitively receptive can leave a person feeling *energetically* drained, especially if they're an empath. You'll know if you're an empath because you will most likely feel fatigued in larger groups of people. This is because you are absorbing small amounts of emotions, pain, and energy from each individual you're around. It adds up to a huge amount of feelings, many of which are not your own.

Here's the scene: let's say you go to a ball game. The stadium is packed. On your left side is a stranger who has major anxiety issues that happen to be flaring up because he has forgotten to take his medication. Sitting to your right is a person who has a history of depression. In front of you is a lady who has explosive anger. Joe Shmo in the seat behind you deals with chronic knee pain because of a high school football injury, and Jane Doe beside him has a severe case of Attention Deficit Disorder.

What does this mean for you, my avid sports fan? It means that if you leave your intuitive switch set to "on," you'll probably leave the stadium feeling anxious, depressed, and angry. Your knee will be throbbing with pain, and you'll have a decreased attention span, all because you absorbed the energy of the people seated around you.

In this sense, yes, being intuitively "on" can leave you exposed to bad energies. But only slightly and only temporarily. It cannot damage your spirit, and after a quick nap you'll feel like a million bucks again.

I want to talk about pasta strainers. You know, pasta strainers, to drain the water from your child's Sponge Bob macaroni and cheese. By the way, I wholeheartedly believe fun-shaped macaroni pastas taste better than the old, boring, elbow macaroni of generations past. Don't you?

Anyway, a spiritual pasta strainer can save you from the bombardment of energy whether you're in a packed stadium of 50,000 people or at your in-laws' family reunion. Try this technique. Before going to the event, imagine a spiritual bubble of protection surrounding you on all sides. Visualize this bubble looking like a pasta strainer. The solid part of the strainer blocks all the bad stuff like other people's knee pain, anxiety, and depression. You can wish these people well and pray for them, but unless you're a professional doctor, counselor, or psychic, there's no good reason for you to feel their aches and pains.

The holes in the pasta strainer, on the other hand, will allow some good energy to filter through to us. People aren't all bad, after all. Some people radiate positive vibes, which is energy you'll actually *want* to absorb and feel.

Are there different types of psychic abilities?

Yes. Loads of them, all different and wonderfully unique. Psychic skills aren't limited to predicting the future and talking with the deceased. Intuition isn't a phenomenon which adheres to the "one size fits all" philosophy. Various intuitives have different abilities.

All mediums are psychic but not all psychics are mediums. Being a medium is a psychic ability that allows someone to communicate with the dead. However, there are other intuitives who do not have this particular gift and are still considered very much psychic.

Clairvoyance is a term that refers to an intuitive who can "see" things, including ghosts and spirit guides. Seeing mysterious balls of light shoot across the room or viewing shadows out of the corner of your eye may be an indication that you're clairvoyant. Viewing energy colors around people (their aura) is also an indication of clairvoyant abilities. Having visions and precognitive daydreams are also tell-tale signs of clairvoyance. I'm sorry to say that it does *not* mean you have x-ray vision and can see through clothing. We'll leave that to Superman.

The term **Clairaudience** refers a person who is able to "hear" sounds using a sixth sense. A person with this ability will often tune in to the chatter of the spirit world. The experience may sound like a laughter-filled cocktail party of voices, driving the intuitive individual nuts and causing her to question her sanity as she tries to fall asleep at night. Those who have learned to harness their clairaudient abilities may be able to tune out the chatter when it's annoying.

Clairsentience refers to an individual who feels the emotions and energy of others on a much deeper level. In my opinion, this is the most common psychic ability, one that all of us possess on some level. People who are clairsentient experience empathy to such an extreme that they can literally feel the aches, pains, and emotions of others. Clairsentience is nearly identical to the "empath" ability I talked about earlier. Although it's hard to distinguish between the two abilities, I'll say that being an empath is like a super-charged version of clairsentience.

Psychometry is the ability to physically and intuitively sense energy from tangible objects. You've probably seen this psychic ability in action before, if you've watched crime shows on T.V. and there was a missing person's case. When the psychic in the show is holding the necklace of the missing person and attempting to locate the helpless abductee, the psychic is using psychometry. The psychic is sensing the energy and vibrations of the missing person, which, over time have worn off on the necklace. Bloodhounds and others dogs with sensitive sniffers can find missing persons with their nose. Some human beings merely do the same thing using their intuition and the gift of psychometry.

Have you ever had a dream that later came true in real life? If so, hopefully it wasn't the one where you're standing naked in your high school hallway and can't get into your locker because you've forgotten the combination. I think we've all had that one, haven't we? Having a dream that later comes true is also known as having a precognitive dream. It's one indicator that you have above-average intuition.

Intuition is like air, and you are the balloon. A balloon expands when you put more air into it, until it eventually pops and releases the pressure. Intuition builds up inside of you when the intuition is not intentionally used. When you have accumulated enough intuition, you "pop," and your psychic abilities inadvertently come out in your sleep as you have dreams of future events. This may sound fascinating, but to the intuitive dreamer, this becomes frustrating, as it's hard to predict which events will unfold in reality and which ones should be ignored as meaningless.

The solution? Actively and intentionally use your intuition when you're awake. How? Trust your gut instincts. Attempt to validate your hunches and feelings. Use your God-given psychic abilities to help someone in need. Tap into your intuition on purpose while you're awake, so it doesn't come out accidentally in your sleep. Pop!

How do I know if I'm intuitive?

All right, we've gotten to know each other well enough that I don't think you'll mind if I ask you some personal questions. I figure I've shared a lot about myself with you already, so, hopefully, you won't mind if we put the spotlight on *you* for a moment. Relax. Go get a pen and a piece of paper (or break out your smart phone or laptop if you're tech savvy). Make a "yes" column and a "no" column. I'm going to ask you ten questions, and I want you to answer them honestly. Keep track and put a tally mark in the correct column. We're going to figure out if you're psychic.

1. Have you ever had a song in your head, and when you turned on the radio, that song was playing? (Exclude the top few most popular songs at that time, which typically get played non-stop all day long).

2. Have you ever known what people were going to say before they said it? (Family members and best friends don't count, since we know them too well and can anticipate what they will say.)

3. Have you ever had a gut feeling that you didn't listen to, and it later came back to bite you in the butt?

4. Have you ever thought about someone you haven't talked to in a very long time, and soon after you thought of them, they called, e-mailed, or texted you out of the blue?

5. Have you ever called someone, and *they* told *you* that they were just thinking about you?

6. Have you ever had a dream that came true?

7. Has your conscience or inner voice ever spoken to you, giving you words of advice or practical guidance?

8. Have you ever had an extremely vivid dream of a deceased loved one in which they looked happy and healthy, and the dream left you feeling comforted?

9. Have you ever seen a ghost, angel, or unexplained energy force?

10. Have you ever looked back on words you recently said and wondered how in the world you came up with such eloquent, wise, and intelligent language? (Inspired from something or someone far more articulate than yourself).

What's the verdict? Are there more tallies in the "yes" column or in the "no" column? **If you have at least two tallies in the "yes" column,** then don't give up hope just yet, my intuitive friend. Your psychic light bulb may not burn as brightly as some others out there, but with enough practice at quieting the self-doubting inner voice that smothers your psychic senses, you should be able to make progress as time goes by. **If you answered yes to at least five of those questions,** then you are moderately psychic and can hold your intuitive head high with pride. **Did you answer yes to seven of the questions?** If so, your psychic balloon is quickly filling up with potential. Use it purposefully and often while you're awake so it doesn't go "pop" in your sleep. **You said yes to all 10 questions, you say?** Then I give you a standing ovation and salute you as a worthy force to be reckoned with in the intuitive community. From one psychic to another, I'm impressed.

Everyone is psychic. That means me, you, your kids, your pets, your boss, and the door greeter at Walmart. Even my childhood friend James had intuition, although he lacked enough common sense to avoid belly-flopping off the high dive on a five-dollar bet in high school. After all, *intuitive* does not necessarily translate to *common sense*. In James' case, ignoring that inner voice of reason resulted in a bright red belly and broken blood vessels around his navel (although, he was five dollars richer!)

Let me get off my high horse here. Don't get me wrong, I've made some bone-headed decisions in my life, ignoring my better judgment and failing to take that little inner voice seriously. How about you? I'd like to hear those stories. Live and learn, right? Being the most intuitive person on Earth doesn't guarantee you'll avoid looking like a jackass from time to time. Trust me. I've been there and done that. *Hee-haw.*

This world is nuttier than squirrel droppings. It's crazy and backwards and scary. God knows this. God would not drop us off here without an inner directional compass called intuition to help keep us on course. It's a tool in the toolbox of our soul which allows us to build a life of happiness. Intuition is innate. It's as natural as breathing. We all have it. Even those who don't believe in psychic abilities *have* psychic abilities. You can call it mother's intuition, gut feelings, a hunch, or a sixth sense, but it's within all of us.

How do I make sure I don't miss signs from my spirit guides or loved ones in Heaven?

You don't have to be in a constant state of spiritual awareness to receive messages. Your spirit guides and loved ones in Heaven are persistent enough and inventive enough that if they want to contact you, they'll get through to you in one way or another. They'll make the message perfectly clear and obvious, just as obvious as the fact that the swerving car in front of you is being driven by a distracted person who thinks updating his Facebook status is more important than the safety of other drivers around him.

While Mr. Busy Thumbs in front of you is inconsiderately texting while driving, your loved ones in Heaven may be trying to get your attention by causing a cardinal (their favorite bird) to fly right in front of your windshield. Or by causing the next song on the radio to be a personally meaningful one to you. Maybe, they'll get your attention by subconsciously causing you to glance at a roadside advertisement which contains one of their names. Or, perhaps, as you're thinking about your deceased loved ones, you see that the license plate on the car in front of you displays their initials and birthdate.

Here's my advice to you: Have clear expectations for your spirit guides and deceased loved ones by letting them know exactly how you want them to contact you. If you want it to be through song lyrics, they can do this by causing us to have a particular song in our head upon waking up in the morning. It's true. Have you ever woken up with a song in your head that you haven't heard in ages? There's usually a reason for this. If you look up the lyrics to that song, the words in it can act as a message from the Other Side, giving you advice, guidance, or clues as to how your day is going to go.

My deceased dad once used music to give a sign to my mom. On what would have been their 35th wedding anniversary, my mom rolled out of bed and silently told my dad, Steve, "I love you honey. Happy anniversary." My mom then left to go to the store. While in the store, she was stupefied to hear a song come through the overhead speakers that she literally hadn't heard in nearly a decade. It was a very rare song that hardly ever gets played, and it happened to be my mom and dad's special wedding song. Overwhelmed with emotions, my mom took this as a sign from my dad that he is doing just fine and wishes her "Happy Anniversary" right back.

Spirits are inventive and innovative when it comes to delivering messages, and music is not the only method they use. Maybe you want your spirit guides or departed family members to visit you in your dreams. Be on the lookout for a sentimental picture on your bedroom dresser to be moved or placed in a different location in your house. These are common occurrences, believe it or not. In my readings, I hear stories like this from my clients all the time. However, I don't want you to feel discouraged if you've been keeping an open mind, looking for signs and messages, but simply haven't been getting them. Trust me, you eventually will. Patience is something we all find difficult. Just keep in mind if the deceased loved one you're hoping to hear from passed away five years ago, that may seem like an eternity for you, but it goes by in the blink of an eye from their perspective in Heaven. Give them some time. They'll deliver a message to you, eventually.

Tell them you want validating signs, but be realistic. If you live in Phoenix, don't ask your dead grandpa to deliver a polar bear walking down the street as a sign for you. Having realistic requests for spiritual messages is just as important as being patient. Keep an open heart and an open mind, but don't be paranoid you'll miss a sign. There is such a thing as looking *too* hard for signs and messages from the universe. I once had a client who said, "I have been seeing spiders all over my house lately, and I'm not sure what kind of message it is. What does it mean?"

I replied, "It means you need to call a pest control person because you have a spider infestation." Not *everything* is a sign. But, I suppose that looking too hard for messages and synchronicity is better than not looking at all.

Please know that there are no coincidences in life, but occasionally, things happen *just because they happen,* and don't necessarily have a metaphysical or other-worldly explanation. It's rare that I come across someone who is putting *too* much thought and energy into looking for spiritual significance. Most of the time when you think someone's trying to contact you, it's because they really are.

Rest assured there is a communication safety net between you and those in spirit trying to contact you. A fail-safe that guarantees they'll get your attention. Have you ever heard your name said out loud by some unseen presence in the room? If you have, then please know you're not crazy. Believe it or not, it's a common experience that a great number of people have. Many clients I talk with admit to experiencing this phenomena at least once in their lives. Why does it happen? Because when all else fails and your spirit guides or loved ones in Heaven cannot get your attention by other means, they will say your name out loud. It's their way of saying, "PAY ATTENTION!"

When this happens, it's startling to say the least. I've had it happen to me before. Yes, even professional psychics and those trained to keep their ears tuned to the spirit world can sometimes be daft enough to miss signs that are right in front of them. I remember drifting off to sleep on my basement couch one time and hearing an urgent whisper in my right ear. "*Andy!*" "Okay, what'd I miss?" I anxiously shouted to my empty basement. I sat there, alert, wide-eyed, and on edge, just like my cat Darwin before he pounces on a toy.

Another time, I was vacuuming the floor when a voice behind me urgently shouted my name, audibly, out of the blue. I nearly jumped out of my own skin, as it caught me off-guard. My heart was pounding faster than a fox fleeing a forest fire. Once I stopped and used my logic, I realized that it wasn't the boogeyman who was out to get me. It was just my guardian angels trying to get my attention. My heartbeat returned to an acceptable sixty-five beats per minute, and I continued vacuuming. I made an effort to be more alert for the remainder of the week, so I wouldn't miss any more signs being delivered to me.

There are countless innovative ways in which those on the Other Side can get our attention. Sleep well tonight knowing you're not likely to miss any important messages or signs from the beyond.

What are the moral obligations of a psychic medium, and what quality of service should I expect from one?

Psychic mediums are essentially middle men. Quite simply, they just relay information. Like a postal service worker, psychic mediums don't create the messages, they just deliver them. You've heard of the phrase "Don't shoot the messenger," haven't you?

Mediums are at the mercy of whatever information is sent from the spirit world, but a good psychic medium will have his psychic antennae tuned to the right frequency and will be able to relay accurate, *specific* information. If he consistently fails to do so, then being a medium may not be his particular strong suit, in which case he would have a moral obligation to forgo that particular brand of intuitive service. Like any profession, skill, or trade, being a psychic medium takes practice, and an intuitive is likely to gain skill, accuracy, and confidence over time the more they train.

Like everyone else, psychics are 100% human and are prone to "off-days," mistakes, and fatigue. It's reasonable to assume that any psychic medium will have good days and great days. However, if a psychic medium is not on top of his game due to fatigue, illness, lack of concentration, stress, or any other reason, he has an ethical obligation to inform his client ahead of time, and/or reschedule the appointment. Keep in mind, this is heavy, emotional, spiritual stuff we're talking about here. Getting a psychic reading (especially a medium session) should be a life-changing and positive experience.

If the cashier at your local grocery store is having an "off-day," she will still be able to ring up your groceries just fine, although she may not be as cheerful or friendly at the check-out counter. No harm there. No problem. However, if your psychic medium is having an off-day and chooses to give you a reading anyway, it can have a profoundly negative effect on you, since receiving a reading is a very powerful and personal experience. Not to mention you'll be spending good money for a *not-so-good* experience.

If you're on the receiving end of a medium session from a psychic, you must be willing to find that happy middle ground of having realistic expectations and at the same time insisting on a quality session. A good and honest psychic medium who has integrity and experience should consistently, accurately, and specifically be able to relay certain information to a client.

A reputable medium should be able to tell you what your loved ones in Heaven have to say about your life and your current events. A quality medium will have the ability to pinpoint certain personality traits and characteristics of your loved ones in Heaven, such as their likes, dislikes, interests, and temperament. If a medium is gifted, they may be able to give you some information involving family heirlooms your loved one in Heaven left behind, knick-knacks they collected, or sentimental items that belonged to them which have been passed down since their deaths. A medium should be able to occasionally identify who else is with your loved ones in Heaven, such as other family members, pets, and friends.

Some mediums are able to pick up on specific names of individuals who have passed away, and I have had some success with this. However, this is by no means a prerequisite for doing medium work, and despite what you may have seen on television "reality" shows, sensing the exact name of a loved one in Heaven is not exactly a common occurrence. I know several psychic mediums who do not specialize in "the name game," and it does not detract from the quality of the work they do.

Let's say you go to a psychic medium hoping to make contact with your Uncle Bobby who passed away. If the psychic says, "I'm hearing the name Bob or Bobby," it may give you a warm fuzzy feeling. On the other hand, if the psychic says, "Your uncle is wanting to mention the time when you two tried to change the flat tire on his truck out in the pouring rain and accidentally locked the keys in the truck," that message would probably have more emotional meaning for you, wouldn't it? It's more specific. In my opinion, the *messages and information* that a psychic medium relays from a person in Heaven is far more meaningful, more important, and more validating than a psychic medium merely sensing the *name* of a deceased loved one.

There are two other important moral issues to keep in mind when seeing a psychic medium. First of all, don't EVER let a psychic hike up the price of your reading half way through the experience. An ethical, professional person will be honest and upfront with you about the rates *before* the reading begins. If they try to force you to buy expensive candles, crystals, or other accessories claiming it will "lift a curse," then run for the hills, my friend. As we discussed earlier, curses and hexes don't exist. If your psychic tries to scare you into spending more money, it proves she is unethical, and personally, I would avoid her.

Secondly, don't ever let a psychic tell you there are demons and dark energies around you. I feel with all my heart and soul that demons *do not exist*. The only demons that are real are those internal demons within us (negative thoughts) that sometimes interfere with our ability to stay positive. With a little effort, these "demons" of anxiety, depression, and self-doubt can be extinguished, and you don't need expensive items from a psychic to do this. There is not a dark presence around you, or anyone else. We are safe, loved, protected, and surrounded by angels.

How much information can a psychic medium get from deceased loved ones?

A medium may channel information from the Other Side in an auditory way, emotionally, visually, or by physical feelings. Personally, when I'm in medium sessions, I use a combination of these various types, depending on my client. Your loved ones on the Other Side are very smart. They know you. They know your strengths, weaknesses, and how you perceive the world. They take this into consideration when they come through with messages during a reading.

Inevitably, I always know if the clients in my office are visual people, because if they are, their loved ones come through with *visual* messages. If, for example, your grandpa in Heaven wanted me to mention the big vegetable garden he used to have behind his house, he would cause me to see images of a large garden in my mind's eye. If you're more of an auditory person and we're connecting with Grandpa, he would simply say "big garden" or "my garden behind the old house."

If your grandpa wanted me to mention the way in which he died, I might physically feel tightness in my chest, indicating a heart attack. If my left knee started to hurt while connecting to your grandpa, it could be his way of mentioning his bum knee that required surgery. Or it could be his way of mentioning the problems *you've* been having with *your* left knee. Our loved ones are always aware of what we're going through, both physically and emotionally. My point is that it's truly an assault on the senses when giving medium readings, and the information coming through has everything to do with my client, for whom the messages are intended.

The process depends on the psychic, and it depends on the loved ones who are coming through. Unfortunately, doing medium sessions is not exactly like having a two-way conversation. It's not a question and answer session with the deceased. I cannot say, "Prove to us that you're here and tell me what your favorite kind of ice cream was." I am at the mercy of whatever they feel like sharing with us in the reading, and I know most other psychics operate like this as well.

Much of the time, messages coming from the departed

are not only validating and sentimental, but downright funny. I once gave a reading to a lady named Barb, who lost her son in 1984 when he was only 12 years old. I *heard* her son coming through and speaking to me (because his mom was more of an auditory processor). Her son told me to bring up "the big fireworks display and the big vacation." This made sense to Barb, and she went on to explain why he would mention this event.

After the family found out her son only had a few months to live, they enrolled him in the Make-A-Wish Foundation, which flew the family to Disney World. While there, the entire family viewed the giant fireworks display, which is a world-renowned specialty of Disney World. Watching that fireworks display was one of the best and last family memories for her son, since he passed away just two months later.

Barb's son then switched from a sentimental message to a funny one, and he wanted me to mention "his stinky shoes." Although you can appreciate my hesitation in doing so, I obliged, and asked her why he was mentioning something about his stinky shoes. She laughed and said she still has the last pair of shoes he ever wore. Barb explained she could not bring herself to get rid of that pair of shoes, so since his death, she's kept them in a basement cabinet. She explained that although her son was not known for odorous feet, that particular pair of shoes was unique. The material of the shoes caused his feet to sweat profusely and made them smell horribly. As odd (and appalling) as this specific message was, Barb really appreciated it. The message provided her with a little validation. He's alive and well in Heaven and knows she's kept his pair of shoes.

Last but not least, her son's final message was a plea for her to finally throw the shoes out so they stop stinking up her entire basement. Barb and I had a good laugh about this. She agreed to do so, since she gets an overwhelming whiff of the shoes every time she walks downstairs.

Other times, our loved ones can communicate through a medium by giving information about things they loved while they were alive. I read a lady named Elaine whose deceased mom wanted me to mention "the peach trees." Elaine then told me when her mom was alive, she would always go on and on about wanting to plant peach trees. Peach trees don't come up in most of our day-to-day conversations, and since the topic was very specific to Elaine's mom, Elaine viewed the message as meaningful. I'm sure her mom is getting to enjoy all the peach trees she can possibly handle in Heaven.

Sometimes, those in Heaven will prove their presence by informing a psychic medium of physical ailments you are currently experiencing. I once met with a nice lady who I'll refer to as Mary. Her late father came through and wanted me to ask Mary how her left hip was doing. Mary confirmed that it frequently causes her inflammation, swelling, and discomfort. At the time, Mary was receiving medical treatment for her left hip. Although her dad can't exactly write her a prescription for pain medication, simply acknowledging his daughter's discomfort in a particular body part is his way of empathizing with her and showing he sees what she's going through.

During the reading, Mary's deceased father also told me that he didn't like to wear formal attire such as suits and ties (not even to his funeral). Mary nearly burst out laughing and said that her dad was not a very formal person. He hated ties and didn't like to wear formal clothes in general. The whole family found it very humorous and appropriate when they buried him in a flannel shirt, so he didn't have to spend eternity in a suit and tie.

Keeping in line with the "what happened at their funeral service" theme, I did a phone session for a grieving lady named Jane who needed some closure from her deceased sister. As Jane and I were talking about her sister's funeral service, Jane's sister wanted me to bring up "the boat docks." On the other end of the line, I could hear Jane choke back some tears as she tried to compose herself. She then explained that her sister's ashes were recently spread just below a particular boat dock where many of her happy memories had taken place. Little clues and hints that our loved ones were at their own funeral service go a long way in reassuring us that they're alive and well, watching us from Heaven.

Occasionally, your friends and family in spirit form will communicate through a psychic medium simply to give you a hard time and lovingly tease you. I met with a young lady named Brittany whose brother had tragically and suddenly died. Intuitively, I heard him telling me to give his sister a hard time about her hair color and the style in which she was wearing it. He said to question why on

Earth she would do her hair like that. Hesitantly, I brought it up, not wanting to offend her, and hoping that she was as good at "taking it" as her brother was at "dishing it out." Did she and her brother have this lovingly sarcastic dynamic of giving each other a hard time? I hoped so. Brittany calmed my nerves by assuring me her brother always went out of his way to "bust her chops" while he was alive. She also explained that the day before our reading, she had cut and colored her hair in a way that she's never worn it before. Gee, thanks bro.

A psychic medium can also relay *compliments* to you from your departed family members and friends. I had met with Gabriella many times before, and I had grown to love not only her gentle nature, but also the way that she used a Spanish-English hybrid in conversation. Truly a kind, compassionate, teddy bear of a human being, if I've ever met one.

Her mom was coming through in spirit with such a strong message I had to interrupt Gabriella and tell her, "Your mom says that she loves your sweater."

Gabriella looked stunned and whispered, "Ay Dios mio." She explained that her deceased mother had the *same exact* sweater she was wearing, only her mom had it in a different color when she was alive. I could feel her mom winking at us from Heaven and giggling that her daughter has the same fashion sense as she had when she was alive. Gracias, Mom.

These are all examples of messages and information a psychic medium is capable of relaying. Again, when you're going into a reading it's important to have reasonable expectations and an open mind, while at the same time insisting on a quality experience. It never hurts to say a silent prayer and ask for your friends or family in Heaven to deliver meaningful messages in your reading prior to it taking place. Most of the time though, my clients' loved ones arrive in my office before my client even shows up. Given the chance, dead people usually have a lot to say. Please don't neglect your own intuition and medium abilities in whatever capacity you possess them. Every now and then, your loved ones will bypass a "middleman" such as myself and deliver a message directly to you. When this happens, appreciate it and hold the experience close to your heart.

If I'm intuitive, does that mean I have to use it to help others?

The way I look at it, if a gift is worth having, then a gift is worth sharing. You don't *have* to use it to help others, but if you do, your intuition will most likely increase in both strength and accuracy. God loves to see us helping one another in any way possible, even if it's by using the psychic abilities bestowed upon us. We all have a responsibility to our brothers and sisters of the human race. It's our civic duty to do the right thing and assist others in need. Not to seek some personal gain, but simply because it's the right thing to do. Using your intuition can be one of many ways in which you can be of assistance to others.

I understand that confidence plays into this. If you're a

newbie to the psychic world, then you may not feel poised to use your intuition for the betterment of others. Give it time. Be patient with yourself. Have faith that even when all the answers in *your* life are not clear, you are still more than equipped to assist others using nothing more than your God-given intuition. I'll let you in on a little secret. Even the most qualified life coaches and professional intuitives don't live a perfect life free from confusion and uncertainty. I don't have *all* the answers, and, sometimes, I make mistakes. I admit I've made errors in judgment when it comes to my own life from time to time.

Just because you're not perfect yourself doesn't diminish your intuitive potential to help *others*. There is no law dictating you *have* to use your psychic powers to assist others. You can keep your intuition to yourself and use it only for personal direction and self-guidance. There's nothing wrong with that. Just keep one thing in mind- if you attempt to use your psychic abilities for selfish or manipulative reasons, then God and your spirit guides will pull the intuitive rug out from underneath you quicker than you can say "lottery numbers."

How psychic can people be about themselves?

Short-term intuition works better than long-term intuition, when we're talking about using your psychic abilities for yourself. You'll come up with nothing but question marks, if you're trying to see ten years into your own future. If you're trying to figure out what's the best course of action to take in the next ten days, you'll have a much clearer intuitive picture. Here are a few examples to show how individuals can have psychic awareness and insight into their own lives.

While reading Kristy, I warned her to be careful and avoid spilling red wine on her white dress at the upcoming family get-together. She thought that was an interesting cautionary message considering the previous night she had a dream that her not-so-nice sister intentionally spilled red wine on Kristy's new white dress. Because of the dream, Kristy had already decided to pack an extra dress, just in case. She was one step ahead of me, intuitively, due to her dream and her sixth sense, and she was as prepared as possible for the wine-filled festivities.

As I was giving a reading to a lady named Theresa, I said her two young boys were really flirting with disaster and needed to be careful not to fall down the stairwell leading from the kitchen to the basement. I could see the layout of her house in my mind's eye, and she validated that the oddly-placed staircase in her kitchen was really a hazard. She explained she had *already* taken precaution to avoid this potential calamity, because her intuition was helping her see into the near future.

These are just a couple of the countless stories that prove I'm not the only intuitive on the planet. Each one of us (including YOU) has a sixth sense, *knowing,* that keeps us on track and out of harm's way. Your intuition is your God-given compass that helps you navigate the seas of life with a little more precision and direction.

If my psychic abilities scare me, can I somehow get rid of them?

If you're not completely satisfied with your intuition, simply return it for a full refund. Just pay shipping and handling. Or maybe God would let you exchange it for in-store credit. I'm just kidding. Kind of. If your intuition scares you, confuses you, or frustrates you to the point of not wanting it anymore, then you are welcome to ask God to turn your intuition off. Yes, you can choose to shut down your intuition for whatever reason. This can be done temporarily, if it's simply too overwhelming for you to handle. Or, your intuition can be permanently shut off if it seems more like a burden than a gift.

How do you turn it off? Simply ask for it to be shut off. It seems almost too simple, but 99% of the time it's an effective technique. The universe offers us intuition as a bonus, a perk, an extra sensory advantage to help us through life, but by no means is it mandatory that you use it. Some people are not comfortable with sensing and feeling things they cannot fully explain. As human beings, we are naturally pre-programmed to fear things we don't understand.

To fully grasp intuition, you must research, read, learn, and identify what your specific intuitive abilities are and how to control them. This takes time and patience. There are countless books (this one included) which help explain how intuition works. My advice to you is to read as much as you can from various sources and hold on to what material rings true for you. Question information that does not seem right to you.

The majority of people who want to shut off their psychic senses are those who are simply overwhelmed by it, like the people who can't sleep at night because of the incessant ramblings of spirit voices in their bedroom. Can you blame them for being irritated with their intuition?

Until you're more comfortable with your sixth sense, feel free to tell the Head Honcho up there that you wish to hit the "pause" button on your intuitive remote control. God understands. You can push "play" later on when you're a bit more confident and educated on the ins and outs of psychic abilities.

Can one person really read the mind of another person?

I was talking to a good friend of mine named Jennifer. We were shooting the breeze about weekend plans. Always wanting to test my intuitive abilities, she jokingly asked if I could sense what she was planning to do with her upcoming weekend. It was a million to one, ridiculous psychic challenge. There were an infinite number of possible activities for her to engage in during the weekend. Figuring the pressure was off me since nobody could possibly make an accurate guess from such a vague question, I blurted out the first thing that popped into my head. "You're going to take a defensive driving course to prevent your insurance from going up due to a speeding ticket."

Not expecting to get any kind of a response out of her, I

bent over to pet her dog. Jennifer blurted out, "How in the hell did you know I got a speeding ticket? And how do you know I'm taking a driving course?"

I stopped petting the dog and looked up at her in disbelief, thinking she was joking with me. "You're kidding, right?" I asked.

Slack-jawed in astonishment, Jennifer shook her head no. I had honestly just been trying to play along and humor her, not trying to make a serious prediction. Yet, somehow, the "random" thought that popped into my head at that instant was the right answer. I did *not* know she had just gotten a speeding ticket, and I did *not* know she was going to take a defensive driving course to prevent her insurance premium from rising.

Did I read her mind in that moment? Given the monumental odds of being able to pick out that particular activity from literally countless others, I'd have to say yes. I did read her mind. Did I do it on purpose? No. Could I do it again at will? I'd have a better chance of being struck by lightning and hitting the lottery on the same day. No, I couldn't repeat that incident of mind reading with Jennifer, on purpose, again in the future. Being psychic doesn't mean a person knows *everything*.

Another example of "mind-reading" happened when I worked at a facility that offers activities for adults and seniors affected by mental illnesses and cognitive limitations. A few of the individuals in my particular group were lower functioning. They were eager for entertainment, and it was my job to provide them with easy and fun activities.

I decided we'd play a game where I pick a random playing card out of the deck and mentally "send" them the image. They attempted to guess which card I was holding. At one point, four different people in a row guessed the *exact card* I was holding. They didn't guess a seven or a king, but a seven of spades and a king of diamonds. Four people in a row! Four different individuals in my group, in succession, defied the 52-1 odds of knowing which card I telepathically sent them. This was amazing! It defied statistics. For the rest of the day, my sweet clients bragged to their peers about the marvelous feat of "magic" we pulled off in our morning card game.

My wonderful clients may have been cognitively limited compared to the average person, but holy cow were they intuitive! We proved that with a deck of cards. To me, it's further proof God is looking out for everyone. When our mental functioning is impaired or people are physically or mentally ill, they are compensated from our great Creator with an extra dose of intuition. It evens the playing field and allows people to navigate their difficult lives a little easier.

Mind-reading is an interesting phenomenon, but I'm inclined to believe that neither myself nor the best psychic on the planet can accurately read minds *consistently* with repetitive and predictable results. Our thoughts are very private. The hardest bone in the human body is the temporal bone, more specifically, the petrous part of it. It's part of our skull. And no wonder it's the hardest bone. It needs to be one fine-tuned, masterfully engineered piece of equipment to house all the brilliant, silly, odd, and ingenious thoughts that bounce around inside our heads every day. If our skulls weren't so thick we'd be susceptible to others reading our minds. But for the time being, I think we're safe. And for the most part, our thoughts will remain private.

I, for one, am grateful that our skulls are the storehouses for our innermost thoughts because I would not want others to be able to read my mind all the time. There are some universal privacy policies put in place by God. Think of it as a HIPAA Federal Privacy Act on a much larger scale. It ensures that our thoughts are *our* thoughts. They belong to us. Not even your spirit guides have permission to eavesdrop on your innermost ideas every minute of the day.

Nevertheless, math professors would remind us, if it's statistically *possible* for something to happen, then given enough time it probably *will* happen. A hiccup in the universal privacy policy allowed me to accidentally read Jennifer's mind, and it allowed my clients to peek inside my head to know which card I held. It was an inconceivably rare loophole in the cosmic fabric, which is not likely to happen again in the foreseeable future. Rest assured, if you visit a psychic, she isn't any more likely to have mind-reading powers than my dog Zico is to recite Shakespeare.

Do our loved ones in Heaven ever get tired of us asking them for messages?

Your four-year-old: How come the sky is blue?

You: Because that's the way God made it.

Your four-year-old: But, why?

You: Because it's the prettiest color, I guess.

Your four-year-old: But how come it's not purple or blue or yellow or licorice red?

You: Because it's always been blue.

Your four-year-old: Can I have some licorice?

You: No, we're having dinner in just a little bit.

Your four-year-old: What are we having?

You: Meatloaf.

Your four-year-old: Can I have licorice with my meatloaf?

You: No, you may not.

Your four-year-old: How come?

You: Because it's not a dinner-time food.

Your four-year-old: Why not?

You: Honey, it's just not. Please drop it.

Your four-year-old (now pouting): I hate meatloaf. Can I have something else?

You: We're having meatloaf as a family. No, you may not have something else.

Your four-year-old: Can we get a hamster?

I can feel your frustration and fatigue already. In a conversation like this, I can also picture you silently smiling because moments like this are priceless and precious. Your four-year-old is not going to remain that age for very long, so you may as well enjoy her curiosity while you can. But as adults, we are prone to exhaustion, especially when bombarded by a rapid-fire succession of constant questioning. The pursuit of knowledge is tiring when you are the one receiving the questions. However, God, your spirit guides, and your loved ones in Heaven do *not* get tired when we constantly ask them for help and insist they make their presence known. And we ask them often, don't we?

Please, God, let me make it to work on time. When am I ever going to catch a break in life? Mom, wherever you are, can you please help me pass this test? Lord, can you help me stay sober for another day? Grandpa, if you're listening, can you please let me figure out what's wrong with my car? God, please give me the strength to make it through this week. Spirit guides, if you're really there, I need you to prove it to me. God, please, oh please let this toilet flush, and if you do I promise to never ask you for anything ever again for as long as I live.

Our spirit guides, our loved ones in Heaven, and God are limitless. And patient. And wise. And compassionately understanding when they hear our desperate pleas for help. Since they do not require sleep in Heaven and are not rushed, stressed, self-absorbed, or mentally checked out, they do not feel stretched too thin when we ask them for help. Therefore, they are not subject to burn-out or impatience when it comes to our asking them for help.

They don't get worn out or frustrated with you even if you ask for help a hundred times a day. They may not answer each prayer every time you ask for it, because it may not be in the best interest of everyone involved to do so. Please know they are listening and won't be annoyed as you beg for patience while making your way down the sugar-filled cereal aisle at the grocery store with your four-year-old. Good luck with that.

Is intuition genetic? Can it be passed down through the generations?

Psychic abilities are genetic. As sure as you inherited your hips from your mother or have your father's eyebrows, intuition is passed on through our genes. So, what does the psychic gene look like? I don't know. I'd like to think it's the part of our genetic code that glows a little brighter than the rest. It's the little sliver of God inside us all. It's the unfathomably powerful part deep within our soul that still knows "who we are" and "why we're here." We all have this shining, shimmering psychic DNA coursing through our veins to a certain extent. It's just a bit more obvious in those of us who come from a long line of family intuition.

I've referred to my Grandma Myers throughout this book. She was my paternal grandmother. She was intuitive and experienced many psychic moments throughout her life. When I was young, she relayed several stories to me hinting that she had frequent, accurate premonitions of future events that later came true. She, eventually, "turned it off" out of fear and frustration. My maternal great-grandmother also dabbled with intuition and I'm told she even read tarot cards for people (well before the time it was socially acceptable to do so).

My mom does not claim to have a lick of intuition. But, in her defense, she is the voice of reason and logic that keeps free-thinking individuals like me grounded. Being so detail-oriented and analytical sometimes stifles a person's intuition and prevents them from tapping into it as often as they'd like. We never got around to talking about psychic abilities when my dad was still alive, so we're not sure what he contributed to the psychic gene pool.

At any rate, my parents must have passed on some quality psychic DNA to both my sister and me. Elizabeth is an intuitive healer. She's able to take away physical and emotional pain from individuals by shifting energy within them. It's unbelievable, really. I lovingly refer to her work as "spiritual oil changes." Countless people have reaped the benefits of her gift, including me. Elizabeth specializes in the health of the body, mind, and spirit, and she is highly intuitive! My older brother, Dave, on the other hand, does not claim to possess any kind of intuition beyond good old-fashioned common sense. Then again, my brother and I discuss intuition about as often as the Pope plays with tarot cards, so perhaps my brother does have some psychic mojo and has simply never told anyone.

But that's how genetics work, right? You may get your mom's blond hair while your sibling gets the reddish hair that runs on your dad's side of the family. Your younger brother may be as slim as a number 2 pencil and your older sister may be full-figured. We're all a blend of the DNA soup from which we sprang. All a product of the genetic lottery from which we bought a ticket. I hope that psychic abilities run in your family tree and that the intuitive branch lands directly on your head.

There are countless variables when we're talking about intuition running in families. I have seen highly intuitive parents have a child who's about as psychic as a door handle. On the other hand, I have seen psychic parents go three for three, consistently giving birth to one intuitive kid after another. You would think that after the third psychic child, you would get one free, right? Like frequent flyer miles or a loyalty punch card.

Conversely, I've had the pleasure of meeting psychic parents who silently shake their heads, wondering why their son lacks enough intuition to refrain from jamming a magenta crayon so far up his nostril it could tickle his brain. We roll the genetic dice and are sometimes surprised at the outcome, aren't we?

Overall, psychic abilities tend to run in families. If you're a descendent of intuitive family members, then it's a bit more likely you'll find the psychic spark buried deep within you. However, it's not a guarantee. As they say, "There are no guarantees in life except for death and taxes." In the meantime, please keep Crayola crayons out of the nostrils of your children if they haven't yet found their intuition and common sense.

Is it wrong to use my intuition for my own purposes?

I don't claim to be the authority for what is *right* and what is *wrong*. And, for that matter, how do we define what is right and wrong? Is it wrong to steal a loaf of bread? What about if stealing that loaf of bread was to feed your family when the alternative was starvation? I'm sure you've heard this philosophy-ridden moral dilemma before. An ethics committee or debate team would love to get to the bottom of this question as it would provide countless hours of free entertainment for everyone involved. I think very few things in life are black and white, right and wrong. I feel most of life resides in that middle, gray area, drifting between the two ends of the moral spectrum.

Don't go reaching for the migraine medicine just yet. I don't want to give you a Socrates-sized philosophical headache. I'm just trying to make a point that most circumstances are not absolutely "right" or "wrong." Sometimes, the answer to a question is "maybe." Is it okay for people to use their psychic abilities on themselves for personal gain? Maybe. In my humble opinion, it would depend on what they're trying to accomplish.

There is nothing immoral about using intuition to help you make decisions regarding your love life, family, career, financial decisions, and your future. Relying on your intuition as a compass to keep you headed in the right direction is not only acceptable, but in fact, advisable. Using your God-given sixth sense to create more happiness and peace of mind is a good thing. Using your psychic senses to become the king of keno or the hero at the horse track is much less advisable, both ethically and karmically. If you're looking for a sure bet, it's that your intuition will increase when used in the right way, and it will decrease if used for malicious or dishonorable purposes.

How do I know if I'm receiving an intuitive message or if it's just my own thoughts?

We have some crazy thoughts, don't we? I know that some of my thoughts border on the bizarre. I don't think we're all that different, you and I. You have weird thoughts pop into your head throughout the day too, don't you? I thought so. What are some of the odd-ball thoughts floating around in the ocean of *your* mind? As for me, I've been wondering why bugs don't die when they fall from great heights.

Think about it. When a lady bug falls off a picnic table, since she is so small, it must be the equivalent of us falling from the Empire State Building. If that were the case, we would go splat. Game over. No doubt about it. How then, can bugs fall from their scaled down version of a tall building and live to tell about it? I think it must have something to do with body weight, the mass of an object, physics, or terminal velocity. Or maybe it has to do with the bug's hard candy shell of an exoskeleton. I'm not sure. Let me know if you've got a good physicist who can shed some light on the matter for me.

Thoughts. Funny little things aren't they? If your mind were a freeway then your thoughts would be zipping around at well over the posted speed limit, changing lanes without signaling, and getting off on the wrong exit. With all the constant chaos and commotion bouncing around in your mind, how is it possible to distinguish an average, every day thought from an *intuitive* thought?

Sometimes, when an intuitive piece of information, in whatever form it takes, enters your mind, it often seems as if it's coming from nowhere. It may catch you off guard. It's as if something came from nothing. It will occur to you as a bit strange, since thinking a thought requires some effort, yet this "inkling" came to you easily, while your mind was elsewhere.

Intuitive thoughts will often enter your brain faster than a lightning bolt in a thunderstorm. Intuitive information tends to pop into your brain quickly because it's truth. The truth is within all of us, waiting to be freed from its chains. The answers to any of life's questions can be found within our intuition. Truth does not need time to think. It simply *is*. Truth is unwavering. It does not go back and forth, just as your intuition will not waver back and forth when it's truly working and actually speaking to you. Truth is instantaneous, just like intuition. The only speed limit on our intuition is the pace at which your mouth can articulate the information you're receiving.

If you're trying to purposefully use your intuition, and information does not come to you quickly and clearly, then you must tap your psychic brakes and not force the issue. There is a big difference between intuition and *imagination*. When you try to force your intuition into working, you'll begin to *make up* information. It's true. Our brains are highly creative instruments. If they're capable of concocting intricate story lines in our nightly dreams, then our brains are also advanced enough to give us false, imaginative information rather than raw psychic messages. If you are waiting for a psychic message to pop into your head and nothing arrives quickly, then be patient and try again the next day. If you plan on using your intuition to help others, you have a moral obligation to give them accurate and honest information. Never, under any circumstance, give a person sugar-coated, make-believe, or potentially inaccurate psychic information because you forced your intuition rather than letting it come to you naturally.

The final clue that will help you distinguish between intuitive thoughts and "regular" thoughts is the *feeling* you get when something crosses your mind. If, when a thought enters your brain, all of your psychic bells, whistles, and alarms go off, then you probably have a code green, full alert, genuine piece of psychic information. If the thought, message, or bit of information floating around in your head *feels* important enough to pay attention to, then it probably is.

Trust information that comes to you quickly and effortlessly. Don't overthink things. Don't force your intuition. Listen to what your gut feeling is telling you. These are all aspects to keep in mind when separating out intuitive information from the heap of other thoughts overflowing from your brain. And, if you see a ladybug, can you ask her how she survived falling off the picnic table? It's driving me nuts.

What is the hardest part of using intuition?

In my opinion, it's communication and timing. Let's start with communication. The English language is embarrassingly insufficient when it comes to conveying intuitive messages. There aren't enough adjectives to do justice to some of the information an intuitive person can sense and feel.

Let's talk numbers. A person who is one hundred percent psychic but has inadequate communication skills will not be nearly as effective as someone who is only fifty percent psychic and fifty percent *poet*. The information intuitive people receive is only as good as their ability to eloquently and descriptively put the information into words that make sense. You could have more psychic abilities than anyone else on the planet, but it really won't make a difference if you're unable to organize the information in your mind, make sense of it, and articulate it.

A lack of proper vocabulary is only half the battle when we're talking about intuitive communication difficulties. The other problem is that you may only receive bits and pieces of the whole psychic picture. For example, when I'm in a reading, I sometimes only "hear" partial phrases or individual words. With such little to go on, it's sometimes hard to know how to interpret it. Luckily, the partial, broken message often means something to my client even when I find it confusing.

For example, one time I was reading a wonderful, young married couple, Angelica and Dan. Angelica's grandmother came through with a message from the Other

Side. Grandma wanted to talk about home improvement projects. I kept hearing the words "bathroom project" and "cabinets."

It's not my job to censor or withhold information that doesn't make sense to me, so I told Angelica and Dan that grandma was mentioning the bathroom and cabinets. This made no sense to me, but it *did* to them. Apparently, they had just recently installed some cabinets above the bathroom toilet for more storage. Whether they knew it at the time or not, Grandma was indeed there to witness the project, and bringing it up during their psychic reading was just her little way of saying she is still aware of what's going on in their lives.

Timing can also be difficult when we're talking about intuition. Past, present, future. Timing is the second thorn in my psychic side when it comes to making predictions and relaying messages from the Other Side. Even when the information I'm sensing, seeing, or hearing is crystal clear, sometimes the timing of the information (when it will happen) is not clear.

Time is perceived differently on the Other Side (in Heaven). Those who are lucky enough to be there don't have clocks, calendars, or watches because they are living in the "now." They are not restricted by the constant ebb and flow of time that binds us on Earth. Therefore, when they give me information for my client, they often include who, what, where, and why, but leave out one important factor, *when*. One day, I was in session with a lady named Heather, and our conversation drifted toward the future health of her husband. Instantly, I received images of him having a black-and-blue toenail from dropping something heavy on it. Without being given additional information about this event, I assumed it hadn't happened yet, and I told Heather, "Your husband needs to be careful not to drop something heavy on his toes in the near future."

Heather put her palms on her cheeks, shook her head, and whispered, "Oh, my God." She then told me that the previous week her husband dropped a manhole cover on his foot while working, and although he didn't consult a doctor, he assumed one of his toes was broken because it turned black and blue, and he was about to lose the toenail.

Heather explained her husband worked for the city, doing road maintenance. Here again, we have an example that intuition is not an exact science, and it never will be. The information I gave her regarding her husband's health was accurate, but the issue of "timing" was admittedly a bit off since I assumed he hadn't injured his toe yet, but in fact it just recently happened.

If you're attempting to increase your intuition or improve on your psychic abilities, I cannot emphasize enough that you must work with whatever information is given to you. Even though the issues of communication and timing are always wild cards in the psychic deck, you must not censor or omit information simply because you cannot make out all the details. Write it down, spit it out, and simply get the information out on the table for you to dissect. If you're relaying intuitive information for someone else, they'll often help you make sense of it.

What are the most unusual ways in which our spirit guides or loved ones in Heaven try to communicate with us?

If coming to us in a dream is too subtle or speaking to us through our inner voice is not proof enough of their existence, our loved ones and spirit guides can throw you a psychic curve ball and grab your attention, using more obvious and creative methods. We've talked about manhole covers and bathroom cabinets, but I've also got a great story about a smiley face on a van.

I was driving out of town to do a psychic show for an audience. I was stressed to the max, at a crossroads in life, and wondering if the Universe had any words of wisdom for me. Cruising down the Interstate, I was praying to my spirit guides, God, my relatives in Heaven, or anyone out there listening who could provide me with some peace of mind.

I remember asking for some comfort. Some validation that everything would be all right. Just as this prayer left my heart at the speed of light and raced towards anyone who was listening, I got my response. I saw my answer. As I said this silent prayer, a van passed me in the left-hand lane. The company van had a giant, yellow smiley face as its logo, and in colossal letters across the side of the van, it read, "Andy's Appliance Repair, Inc."

Seeing my name on the side of the van along with the incredibly large and in-charge smiley face gave me hope. It provided me with comfort. It reminded me that everything happens for a reason, and these messages of love are delivered in the strangest and most unexpected ways, as long as we're looking for them.

As the big van began to pass me and speed ahead on that cold afternoon, a big smile came across *my* face. I noticed the company slogan near the yellow smiley face, which read, "We've got you covered." Who was the message coming from? Who caused that van to pass me on the Interstate with such impeccable timing? God? The Universe? My spirit guides, my dad, or maybe my grandma? I thanked them all just to cover all my bases. Tears welled up in my eyes, as I barreled down Interstate 80 toward my show. My tension melted away, knowing that "I was covered" by a higher power, and everything in my life would be okay in the long run.

Smiley faces on vans are one of a million ways messages can be conveyed to you from an invisible, loving presence. From the spiritually significant to the simplistically silly, messages come in all shapes and sizes. I gave a reading to a young lady named Lauren who wanted to connect with her deceased grandfather. He gave me an interesting message.

I said to Lauren, "Your grandpa says you'll hear whistling sounds when he comes around and visits you."

She breathed a sigh of relief, as she slouched down in her chair and grinned widely. Lauren said this was validating, and she was happy to know she wasn't losing her mind after all. She told me that just a few days before her session with me, she was at home, thinking about her grandpa and missing him dearly, when all of a sudden she heard a whistle, loud and clear. Nobody else was home at the time, and for the life of her, she couldn't figure out where the whistling sound could have originated.

Along with audible whistles from the afterlife and inspiration on the interstate, messages can come in the form of physical items being moved by unseen forces. One of the most fascinating and awe-inspiring stories I've ever heard came from a client of mine, who is a sweet older lady in her seventies named Ruth.

In our session, Ruth told me her husband, Fred, had been deceased for many years. When they were younger, Fred bought her a pair of earrings, which, over time, had become very important to her. Like many sentimental gifts, they became too precious to risk losing after Fred's death, and so after he died, Ruth kept the earrings tucked away in a box underneath her bed. "They remained there for several years, untouched by anyone," she explained to me.

On what would have been a milestone wedding anniversary for them, Ruth walked into her bedroom and nearly fainted as she spotted that special pair of earrings resting perfectly on the pillow of her neatly made bed. Can you imagine the joy, sorrow, surprise, and wonder she must have felt, standing there alone in her bedroom, staring at those earrings? It gives me goose bumps thinking about it. It inspires me.

Stories like this are heartwarming to say the least. Although rare and cherished, they really DO happen. It shows that our loved ones and spirit guides can and *do* use creative ways to communicate with us. I am convinced Fred was there to celebrate that milestone wedding anniversary with Ruth. Although not with her physically, he was somehow able to move a physical object from underneath her bed to leave her utterly amazed. A unique and memorable anniversary gift if there ever was one.

Keep your eyes open, my friend. Keep your ears and your heart open, as well. Whether it's through objects in our physical surroundings, an animal, our inner voice, in dreams, or delivered through another person, we all get messages from those in spirit form who love us.

Andy, what is the most interesting sign you've ever gotten from a guardian angel or deceased family member?

Once upon a time, I drove a sporty little five-speed stick shift. There was one weekend when my car overheated. The needle on my dashboard pointed straight to the "H," indicating my engine was hotter than Death Valley in August. I pulled my car to the side of the road every mile or so, letting it temporarily cool down. Finally, I made it home and parked my car in the garage. Logic dictated I shouldn't drive it again until Monday morning, when I would take it straight to my mechanic. Sunday evening rolled around, and I was desperate for a few essential food items for dinner. I knew it was a bad idea to drive my car and that it would probably overheat again, but I pushed my luck and attempted to leave anyway.

As I turned on my car and put it in reverse to back out of

the garage, my garage door suddenly closed all by itself. In disbelief, I looked down at the garage door opener which was resting on the passenger seat. I had not bumped it or accidentally pushed the button. Apparently there was someone or something trying to prevent me from leaving. Being the hard-headed, stubborn mule I was, I re-opened the garage door and backed out of the driveway. I made it to the gas station up the street to get my essential grocery items. My car did not overheat again. "So far, so good," I thought to myself.

As I attempted to drive out of the gas station parking lot, I heard an unexpected clicking noise coming from the center console of my car. I glanced down and noticed the parking brake handle had just been raised, though only seconds earlier, I had lowered it to disengage the parking brake. Thinking it was a bit odd, I disengaged the parking brake a second time by pushing in the button and lowering it. As I tried to leave the parking lot, I once again heard "click, click, click, click." Shaking my head in disbelief, I looked down to see my parking brake had been raised yet again by an unseen hand. I was the only person in my vehicle!

Defying this warning and determined to make it back home, I slammed the parking brake back down and began to drive off slowly. This time, I kept my eyes fixed on the parking brake. As sure as the sky is blue, I watched in awe as the parking brake lever defied gravity and elevated on its own accord to a fully engaged position. "Click, click, clickety, click." Whether it was an angel, Grandma Myers, or my spirit guides, there was some invisible presence in my vehicle that was trying to tell me not to drive my car. My only other option was to walk home, so I decided to disengage the parking brake for the fourth time and high-tail it back home. I made it to my house safely, without my car overheating.

Later that night, around three o'clock in the morning, I woke up to use the restroom. Upon walking back into my bedroom, I noticed an object on the floor that just didn't belong. My vision was fuzzy, and the room was dark, so I couldn't make out what the heck the strange object was in the middle of my bedroom floor. I flipped on the light and focused my eyes. Exhaling in sheer bewilderment, I saw the object was a framed picture, which usually hangs on my bathroom wall. The picture displays a quote which reads, "He who is one with himself is one with the universe."

Cue the *Twilight Zone* music (Do dee do dee, do dee do dee). At the time, I slept with my bedroom door closed, so I didn't understand how a physical object such as a picture could have magically teleported through my wooden bedroom door onto the floor. There was nobody else in my house that night, and I have never been prone to sleep walking, so I ruled out those two possible explanations.

Finally, 9:00 a.m. arrived. The previous night was strange to say the least. I drove my car straight to my mechanic's shop as planned. A few hours later, the shop called me to give me an update on my car. "Well, your engine is working perfectly fine," I was told. "There's no reason on Earth why your car should have overheated," she said. In my mind, I replayed the unexplained events of the previous night: my garage door closing, the parking brake incident, and the moving picture. What did it all mean?

I turned my attention back to the lady on the phone. "So, your engine is in perfect working order, but we did find some major problems with your brakes."

"What kind of problems?" I asked.

"Well, let's just say that if you hadn't brought your car into the shop today, you would have gone to hit the brakes, and you wouldn't have *had* any brakes." She and her husband were family friends, and I had taken my car to their shop for years. If they said my brakes were bad, I trusted their honesty. She chuckled and explained to me how it was my lucky day. "The repairs might cost you a pretty penny, but at least you'll live another day."

I refrained from asking her what could cause a parking brake to engage itself several times in a row without the assistance of a human hand. I smiled, as I thought to myself, there probably wasn't a diagnostic tool in their shop to explain it. I felt comforted in knowing that someone, somewhere, was looking out for me. I'm not sure who it was protecting me that wonderfully weird weekend, but I'm glad that spirit caused my car to overheat, which in turn led to the discovery of the major problem with my brakes.

I'm also grateful that ignoring the obvious signs did not lead to a car accident. The next time my garage door closes me inside my garage or my parking brake tells me not to drive my car, I'll listen. As to why the bathroom picture relocated itself that strange evening, I may never know.

This next story is wonderfully odd, as well. When my wife and I moved out of the house where Grandma Myers once lived, we welcomed Grandma to follow us in spirit and fill our new digs with her wonderful energy. A few days after moving into our new home, Grandma gave us the strangest sign, proving she's still with us in spirit. In our sitting room, there's a big picture window. Above the window sits a cornice box. For you youngsters out there who might not know what a cornice box is, it's a padded, decorative thingamajig that rests above the window and the drapes, kind of like a six-feet long, sideways rectangle. It weighs a good five to ten pounds.

A few days after my wife, Kenzie, and I settled into our new home, I walked into the sitting room and froze, as I viewed an odd sight. The cornice box, that earlier in the day was centered above the picture window, now rested vertically against the wall, behind a lamp, several feet away from the window. It was like someone intentionally took it down, moved it to the side, and carefully stood it end-over-end, behind the lamp in the corner. There is no way on God's green Earth it could have fallen in this manner. It's heavy and awkward, and even if it did fall from atop the window on its own, it would have ended up lying horizontally on the ground, not vertically propped up against the wall.

After asking my wife if she took it down, and checking with my mom, sister, and anyone else who could have had access to our house, we discovered nobody had played a practical joke on us. Everyone swore they did not touch the cornice box. There was no explanation. At this point, I recalled that prior to our move, we asked Grandma for a sign that she was moving into the new house with us. We concluded this was her inventive way of telling us she was there.

I hope you like the new house, Grandma! It's not filled with your memories, and it doesn't smell like your scent. But we promise to make our own memories here, and we'll fill it with wonderful and loving energy.

Chapter 6: Reincarnation and Past Lifetimes

Is there any proof that we have lived past lifetimes?

I was giving a reading to a lady who we'll call Margaret. While discussing her past lifetimes with her, I received images of her being in Venice, Italy. She was a male in that lifetime, and one of her jobs was to stand at the back of the gondolas with her long oar, and steer the boats through the canals of the city. Sounds romantic. Sounds like a good job, huh? Only problem was Margaret enjoyed her wine a little too much in that lifetime. She was known to tip back a few too many Pinot Grigios before work. It affected her ability to navigate the boats to the correct destination, and more importantly, it affected her *balance*! As you can imagine, not falling off your gondola was most likely a prerequisite for the job.

In my mind's eye, I could see the scene unfold. Drunken Margaret falling off the back of her gondola and crashing into a nearby staircase, severely injuring her left shoulder. Funny? Perhaps. Sad? Maybe a little. Her left shoulder gave her problems for the rest of that particular lifetime and affected her ability to steer the gondolas. After I explained this to Margaret, she shared something very interesting with me. She told me a few years prior to our reading, she unexpectedly and mysteriously developed moderate pain in her left shoulder. It came on suddenly and did not stem from any known injury. Her shoulder pain in this current lifetime became significant enough to interrupt her daily activities. At the time of her reading with me, Margaret was seeking the advice and care of medical professionals and trying to get the shoulder pain under control.

Cell memory is a term that refers to past life baggage that somehow carries into this lifetime. Sometimes, it's a phobia, and sometimes, it manifests as an unexplained pain. In other cases, it's a fondness and obsession with a certain place or event. Was Margaret experiencing cell memory when her left shoulder once again caused her pain? Typically, cell memory occurs in this lifetime at the same point in time, or same age, as the incident occurred in a past lifetime. For example, if Margaret injured that left shoulder at age 30 in Venice, Italy, it could correlate to her suddenly feeling shoulder pain at age 30 in this current lifetime.

From Italy, we now move to Peru in South America. Have you ever heard of Machu Picchu? Weird name. Amazing place. It's situated high in the mountains above the Urubamba Valley in Peru. Machu Picchu consists of the ruins of an Incan civilization that thrived until the 1500s. With its green, rolling hills and multi-leveled plateaus, it looks as majestic as it does mysterious. When you view pictures of this eerie landscape, it looks as if a dinosaur could be looming around every stone wall. Truly the "land before time."

This was the site of a past lifetime for one of my clients named Amy. As always, the images came to me in my mind's eye, like clips from a movie trailer, and I relayed to Amy what I saw. I pictured her travelling through the ruins of Machu Picchu a few hundred years ago with a group of people who were interested in pushing forward in search of valuables and food. Amy wasn't at Machu Picchu for long in this past lifetime, but she was sick to her stomach the entire time she passed through it. Nearly doubled over in pain, Amy pressed on, occasionally clenching her stomach, while she experienced intense nausea.

After relaying these past life images to Amy, I asked for her feedback (not necessarily expecting her to relate to such an odd past life experience). She took a deep breath and when I saw a hint of a smirk on her face, I knew she had something to say.

"It's funny you mention this, because I have actually been to Machu Picchu, just a few years ago," Amy said.

Unable to practice restraint, I blurted out, "Are you serious?" I didn't mean to sound too surprised, but at the same time, I thought a remote mountain in Peru is not exactly somewhere you would expect many people to have visited.

The most interesting part was how Amy *felt* while at the ruins of Machu Picchu just a few years prior to our reading. She experienced nausea. Extreme upset stomach. She was doubled over in pain, trying not to vomit. This illness came on suddenly and unexplainably, while at the ruins of Machu Picchu. Amy felt fine over the course of the trip leading up to and after Machu Picchu, but for some odd reason, she was sick the entire time her group visited the ancient ruins (just like in her past lifetime).

We've visited Italy and Peru, so let's continue to hop continents and land in Africa, where I want to share another experience that lends possible proof of reincarnation. I gave a reading to a lady named Roberta. She was a male in this past lifetime, and lived in a Central African country. She was a medicine man of sorts, whose job was to provide herbal remedies and spiritual healing for her community.

In this past life vision, I clearly saw Roberta (the medicine man) develop a strange condition over time affecting her right hand. It curled up and contorted into a claw-like shape. The hand got worse over time and eventually became stiff and unusable, but it did not deter Roberta from continuing her work of healing and spiritual guidance for her community.

As I described this to Roberta, she stopped me mid-sentence, and held out her right hand. At first, I was puzzled, since there was nothing unusual about her hand. She pointed out that her right hand appeared normal. Her fingers were straight, and she had good mobility. I noticed nothing abnormal.

She continued, "For the past few years this right hand

randomly and annoyingly contorts and curls up from time to time." She said when her hand locks up and becomes like a claw, it's so stiff she can't even hold a toothbrush. She told me she is working with physical therapists to determine a diagnosis and to alleviate the condition to make her hand more mobile on a consistent basis.

My heart goes out to Roberta, and I hope her doctors *can* find a cause, a diagnosis, and a prescription to get the condition under control. I have a sneaking suspicion that the root cause of this weird anomaly may be directly linked to Central Africa and a medicine man from a few hundred years ago.

We've talked about a dislocated shoulder in Italy, an upset stomach in Peru, and a clawed hand in Africa. Rest assured, not all past life cell memory cases are negative. There are also positives that carry through from one lifetime to another.

Let me tell you a story about a horse. I was in a reading with someone named Kim. Once again, the reincarnation flood gates were opened, and I felt the waters of her past lifetimes wash over me like a cold shower. I described these images to Kim as they entered my mind. I saw Kim working as a cowboy in Colorado, surrounded by horses. I sensed that in this past lifetime, she always felt the strongest bond with white horses that had brown spots.

After telling Kim all of this, she opened up and began to share a little bit about herself. "First of all," she said, "my family lives in Colorado and since I visit them often, I feel a special connection to Colorado." Kim also divulged she has worked with horses in this current lifetime, and she is drawn to one particular type. You guessed it, white horses with brown spots! She forms the best relationships with horses that have this coloring, and admits to having a fondness for them. Some of our likes and preferences can spill into our current lifetime from the past, apparently even our connection to a particular type of horse.

So, is there proof behind the concept that past lifetimes are real? You decide. Personally, I've seen people believe much more ridiculous concepts based on much less proof. I believe our existence is circular, not linear. Round and round we go on this cosmic roulette wheel. Your soul is eternal, and you have lived on this Earth before. Your soul cannot be damaged by pain or heartache. You are an infinitely wise being who has a rich and interesting history. You have witnessed the best and the worst of what the human condition has to offer. The experiences you encounter from lifetime to lifetime remain in the warehouse that is your soul.

How many lifetimes do we have to live before we are done incarnating?

Sixty-three. Once you live sixty-three lifetimes, you can retire and spend the remainder of eternity resting your weary soul in Heaven. Actually, I'm completely kidding. I just wanted to make sure you're still paying attention and took my advice about questioning things that sound silly or false or don't ring true for you. Congratulations on not being gullible. I reward you with the Reincarnation Badge of Logic.

How many lifetimes do we have to live before we're done? The answer to this question is different for everyone. No soul has to live a predetermined number of lifetimes before it is done incarnating. The amount of lifetimes people live on Earth is subject to change, based on a few factors: what they have already learned from their past lifetimes, what they hope to learn in the future, how thoroughly they learned their life lessons, and how much wisdom they wish to acquire. Nobody else is in control of how many times we incarnate. Not God, not our spirit guides, not even angels. Only you are in control of your evolution.

What does the term "old soul" mean?

Ask statisticians, and they'll assure you numbers don't tell the whole story. While in college working toward my Bachelor's Degree in Social Work, I had to take a statistics class. The only thing I remember is "quantitative" has to do with the numbers of a study. The hard facts. The math. On the other hand, the term "qualitative" means the story behind the numbers. It means the missing pieces, the intangibles, and the part of the calculations that can't necessarily be measured with numbers. Although we have lived a very definitive and precise number of past lifetimes, what qualifies us as an old soul is not the number itself, but the *life experiences* we've had.

An old soul is someone who has accumulated a lot

of wisdom from past lifetimes. Old souls demonstrate certain telltale personality traits, which may include exceptional kindness, elevated intuition, independence, and self-sufficiency. They have the ability to keep things in perspective, because they are spiritually evolved. They have a good sense of direction in life, are highly empathetic, passionate, and emotionally deep. Old souls show talent in a wide array of skills and are interested in a diverse range of hobbies and activities.

Does this sound like you? If so, I award you one gold star. I congratulate you, as you have joined an exclusive club called Wonderfully Incredible old Souls for Enlightenment, also known as WISE.

Actually, this elitist club doesn't exist. I made it up. What's life without imagination and creativity? If that club was real, wouldn't you want to be president? I'd nominate you. On a serious note, if the previous description fits you for the most part, then in truth you probably *are* a wise, old soul. If you've thrown this book across the room in frustration because the description above does *not* describe you, then I have two things to say. First of all, shame on you for throwing your book. Secondly, and most importantly, go easy on yourself. Not everyone is an old soul (yet), and besides, it's not a race anyway. We're all going to get to the finish line we've put in place for ourselves. All of us will evolve into the best person we can be. Old souls are not more special than younger souls. Neither person is less valuable or more amazing in the eyes of God. We all have our place in this wonderfully weird and wacky world.

Going back to what I learned in statistics class, numbers don't tell the whole story. The person who has lived twelve past lifetimes could possibly exhibit more traits of an old soul than another person who has lived forty past lifetimes. There are three key factors in determining a person's "old soul-ness."

First of all, how long did you live in each of your previous lifetimes? Did you exceed your life expectancy or die young? If you were to die at age six, you obviously won't have the time to soak up wisdom and knowledge like you would if you died at age sixty. Simple logic dictates that more years on Earth allows for more experiences. More experiences mean more growth.

The second factor in evolving into an old soul is the difficulty of each lifetime you have lived. The more challenging a lifetime, the more a person grows from it spiritually. We accumulate priceless traits: resiliency, strength, perspective, and depth of character. Therefore, a poor peasant would be *more likely* to gain wisdom at a faster rate than a pampered princess. Remember this rule of spiritual evolution, and keep in mind that a difficult life means a beneficial life in terms of wisdom and growth.

The third and final factor in molding yourself into an old soul is the speed at which you learn life lessons. The faster you embrace and learn your life lessons, the faster you evolve. Being a fast learner frees you to work on more life lessons, allowing you to improve more aspects of yourself. Simply put, a person who doesn't have to learn everything the hard way is free to grow and evolve at an alarming and wonderful rate, like a snowball growing as it rolls down the hill.

So, who holds the record for living the most past lifetimes, and who is the oldest soul? I knew you were going to ask that! Americans love competition, don't we? We love statistics and records and want to know who is top dog. In terms of sheer wisdom, the jury is still out. All I can say for sure is that it's not me! Although we can talk about traits and characteristics of an old soul, it's hard to *qualitatively* measure who is the wisest. In terms of sheer numbers, I've never given a reading to a person who I felt lived more than 53 past lifetimes. On the other end of the spectrum, I've never met anyone who has lived fewer than seven previous incarnations.

How do I know when it's my last lifetime?

Every once in a while, I'll find myself giving a reading to a client, and I'll intuitively sense it's their last lifetime here on Earth (their last incarnation). After hearing this from me, they raise their hands in celebration and exhale a "Thank God!" With a smile, they agree with me and state they've always felt like it was their last lifetime. They are relieved there's a finish line in sight. These old souls go on to assure me they're not suicidal, pessimistic, or dislike being alive. On the contrary, these individuals are usually happy, compassionate, do-gooders who have left a positive stamp on the world. They're thrilled to hear it's their last lifetime, simply because they're tired. They're exhausted from countless lives filled with emotional and physical adversity.

If it's your last lifetime, you'll likely feel it in your soul. The feeling is similar to the aftermath of a heart-pounding and sweaty workout. Your muscles will ache, and your joints will hurt, but you'll feel an uplifting sense of satisfaction. It's the kind of hurt that feels good.

This is called spiritual fatigue. I didn't invent this term, but I'd like to shake the hand of the person who did, because it perfectly describes what you'll feel if you're nearing your last lifetime on Earth. The trials and tribulations we experience from lifetime to lifetime can build up inside our spirit, stored in the never-ending and eternal lockbox of your soul. Although we essentially have a fresh start from lifetime to lifetime in terms of our appearance, memory, location, family, and place in the world, all of our past life experiences are still very much tattooed on our soul.

If, for example, you've already lived 33 past lifetimes, it's truly staggering to imagine all of the experiences you may have encountered along the way. Perhaps, you were married 33 different times and have had your heart broken even more times than that. In these past lifetimes, you would have most likely fractured dozens of bones in your body. You would have endured the trauma of being born 33 times and dying 33 times. You, in one incarnation or another, have probably been drowned, hung, shot, trampled, imprisoned, and enslaved. In your more memorable past lifetimes, you've no doubt played the role of hero and saved countless lives. You've had 33 fathers and 33 mothers, not to mention other parental figures who were not related by blood. You have won awards. You have been both rich and poor. If you've lived 33 lifetimes and had, on average, two children in each life, it means you've mothered or fathered approximately 66 children. Feeling overwhelmed?

Keep in mind, many of my clients have lived *more* than 33 lifetimes, which means the figures I mentioned above may be a bit conservative. Spiritual fatigue. It's real. And it's a key contributing factor to our decision about whether or not to come back to Earth again for another incarnation. For years now, I've sworn this is my last lifetime. My last stop. Of course, this decision is subject to change. It all depends on what I accomplish while I'm still here, which brings me to our next topic.

Have you ever run a marathon? Maybe a half marathon? We can compare our succession of lifetimes to the miles that roll by as you run a marathon. There are "good miles" and "bad miles." There may be times when you mentally struggle to stay focused. At other points during the race, you contemplate giving up. Maybe at mile number 19 you feel a leg cramp coming on, but somehow push through. Ask marathon runners, and they'll tell you that ideally, you want to sprint across the finish line to end with the best possible time. This is possible if you've saved enough energy and if you've stayed mentally disciplined.

Other times, fatigue gets the best of you, and you're lucky to cross the finish line at a slow walk or *at all*. If this is truly your last lifetime here on Earth (the last mile that you're running), be sure to sprint across the finish line. End the race as strongly as possible, even if you collapse in a heap afterwards.

If it's your last lifetime, this means getting the very most out of each moment. Squeeze every last drop out of the human experience by appreciating the little things in life, while at the same time, keeping everything in perspective. Appreciate every breath, every tear, every laugh, and every interaction with all of the special souls who cross your path throughout the day. Overcome your fears and don't avoid them. Watch less television and spend more time discovering yourself. Push through insecurities. Improve on your weaknesses *and* your strengths. Give away kindness like fruitcake after Christmas. Sleep less and do more. Experience the world in all its beauty, chaos, and wonder. Sprint across the finish line. If you can do this, then, perhaps, you're on your last incarnation.

Are we always the same gender from lifetime to lifetime?

One evening I came home from work, kissed my wife, and asked her what she had been doing in the hours since she had been home. Come to find out, she had gone to the hardware store to get parts for our broken toilet, fixed the broken toilet, changed all the burned out light bulbs in the house, took out the trash, and even fixed a loose kitchen cabinet door that had been hanging on for dear life for the past few weeks.

Maybe, she was fueled by an extraordinary amount of

caffeine on that particular day, but I have to admit that my wife is more inclined to handle the household handy projects than I am. Kenzie has been male more times than female in her past lifetimes. Men were expected to play the role of "fixer" and "builder" throughout history; therefore, my wife had more opportunities to acquire these skills. It makes her slightly more mechanically inclined in her current life, and the skill set comes naturally to her.

Yes, I am fully aware that women are just as capable and competent as men, when it comes to fixing a toilet, taking out the trash, or doing a multitude of home improvement projects. These chores are fair game for both husband and wife in every marriage, yet, traditionally and historically, the fix-it projects have defaulted to the husband. Is it something built into a husband's DNA, stemming back to his hunter-gatherer days?

Here's the iconic image: chest puffed out in pride, husband fixes anything that is broken. His tool belt displays various weapons of choice. Hammers. Screwdrivers. Pliers. Tape measure. Husband claims the garage, basement, or shed as his territory to house all the parts and nuts and bolts and belts and filters and wires and doohickeys that he needs to "fix it." Fueled by testosterone and his will to be a good provider for his wife, husband fixes everything that needs to be fixed, and by god, he fixes a few things that did *not* need to be fixed, making matters worse. Historically, traditionally, this is essentially how it's been for millennia.

Not in my house. Not us. I'm not sure exactly when it

happened, but somewhere along the way, I lost the will to pretend I'm a manly, tool-savvy guy. I lost my instincts to be the dominant alpha male. I also lost all those nuts and bolts and tools and doo-hickeys that you need to fix things around the house. "Last time I saw it, it was in the basement drawer somewhere" has become my trademark phrase around the house. Then again, I have been female more times than male in my past lifetimes. Although in present times, it's more common and more acceptable for women to be handy, throughout history this hasn't been the case. I didn't have as many opportunities to acquire this particular skill set. Nowadays, I'm less inclined and less interested in any project that involves constructing or repairing something.

I believe that just because a woman is good at fix-it projects and knows her way around the inside of a garage, it does *not* make her manly. I also agree that being sensitive and emotional does not make a man any *less* manly. However, the amount of times we've lived as either gender in past lifetimes can contribute to our demeanor in this current lifetime. Tom may be more comfortable drinking a latte and talking about relationship issues, while Tina might feel more inclined to drink a beer and work on a car engine.

Sometimes, I find myself giving a psychic reading to a woman who appears to be very feminine. Hair immaculately colored and cut. Manicure and pedicure freshly done. Designer brand purse. Earrings. Make-up. Wearing a stylish dress and a hint of perfume. However, when I access information about her past lifetimes, it's a different story altogether. Sometimes these darling divas have actually lived more past lifetimes as male, not female. When this is the case, a woman may still be influenced by male energy from the past, and although very feminine in this lifetime, she might find it easy to get along with the guys in her life.

During these readings, when I explain this to my estrogen exuding client, she typically agrees with it wholeheartedly and reports that she's always gotten along better with guys but finds it difficult to be around a group of women for any length of time. She's more comfortable tailgating at a football game than she is at a bachelorette party. On the flip side, if a guy has lived more past lifetimes as a female, he'll most likely take it in stride when he finds himself included in Friday evening's "girls' night out."

I believe all of us have both masculine and feminine traits residing in us. Balance is the key. Tapping into both aspects of our being can be difficult but it's essential for the complete human experience. Logic and emotion, brute strength and delicate finesse, connectedness and independence, attention to detail and big picture perspective, tough love and gentle understanding. All of these dichotomies have their place in the world, and thanks to the feminine and masculine perspectives, we can each express both.

To make a complicated subject very simple, the gender we've been in past lifetimes *does* affect us presently. Those heavily influenced by feminine energy will be more inclined to access the feminine traits, and those who have been male more often in past lifetimes will feel compelled to play the role of provider and fixer (sometimes breaking things in the process that were in good working order before being "fixed").

Do our same friends and family members incarnate with us from lifetime to lifetime?

Yes, sometimes our friends and family members in our current lifetime have been with us, in some capacity, in the past.

Do you have a friend whom you don't see as often as you'd like, but find whenever you happen to get together, you pick up right where you left off? You feel connected to her, an unspoken familiarity. I'll betcha $10 that you've shared a past lifetime with that particular friend. This explains the connection. Some of us have known each other in the past, and this can strengthen our connection in the present.

Some people refer to this phenomenon as "soul groups." Although your friends, family members, and enemies can be linked to you in past lifetimes, the roles in which they play in your life may change from one incarnation to the next.

For example, your mom in this lifetime may have been your cousin in a previous lifetime. Your boss may have been your brother last time. And who was previously your friend in a past life may currently be your husband. I once read a lady named Jean who I felt shared a past lifetime with her daughter, Amber. However, in the past lifetime the roles were reversed, so that Amber was the mother and Jean was the daughter. After I told her this, Jean let out a belly laugh and said, "Maybe that explains why Amber is so bossy and always insists that she knows what's best for me even though she's only five years old."

What is karma, and how does it relate to reincarnation?

Karma is giving and receiving. It means playing the villain and the hero. It means having the total, cumulative human experience by being on both ends of each imaginable situation throughout our incarnations. Karma doesn't mean an eye for an eye. Karma is not payback. It is not retribution, and it's not retaliation from an angry God who wants to see we get what's coming to us. Karma is planned into our life chart by us and others involved in our lives, so that everyone gets to experience all that the world has to offer. Simply put, karma is cosmic balance on the grandest stage.

Most karma is fulfilled within one given lifetime. One example is an out of control, Tasmanian devil of a child who grows up and has a child of her own who is a handful to deal with. By the way, this scenario always makes grandparents smile. Many years ago, when they said, "I hope you have a child exactly like you," they were inadvertently talking about karma. Again, the universe is not punishing the mom by blessing her with a rambunctious little free-spirit of a child. But, for that mom to fully and completely understand the parent-child relationship as far as hyperactivity is involved, she must be on both ends of the spectrum. She will understand how it feels to be the hyper child *and* the fatigued parent trying to keep up with the kid.

There are as many examples of karma as there are stars in the sky. To understand life's inconveniences, a person might inadvertently *cause* a fender bender car accident and later be on the receiving end of one. To understand the messy parts of love and relationships, a woman may cheat on her significant other and then *be cheated on* sometime down the road. To understand and master various aspects of competition, you may experience the heartache of 2nd place while losing in the championship game, then feel the sheer exhilaration of winning the title in the following season. In one way or another, we'll all experience both sides of each situation throughout our existence on Earth.

Karma is when you're shorted one cheeseburger in a fast food drive-through and years later, to your delight, you find an extra order of fries in your bag. Karma is helping your friend move into a new apartment and years later having him help you move into your new house. It's the helpless feeling of being cared for that one time when you threw out your back, and it's the time you stayed up all night caring for your daughter as she was sick and vomiting.

Give and take. Up and down. Good and bad. Selfish and selfless. Helping and being helped. Karma is the balance in life. Karma does not favor some and look down on others. Karma is static. It just *is*. Without it, we would be limited in our human experiences. Karma is both sides of the coin. Speaking of coins, have you ever taken a penny or left a penny in the little dish at the checkout counter in the store? It's sometimes referred to as the "karma cup."

Do some of our likes or dislikes from past lifetimes still affect us now?

Yes, but first let's look at this topic from a scientific point of view. In the psychology community, the debate continues about whether a person is influenced more by genetics or by the environment around them. This is the age old "nature versus nurture" debate. When we interlace this argument with talk of past lifetimes, a person may wonder if little Patrick is fascinated with trains because his favorite uncle also loves trains (and therefore has influenced Patrick), or if Patrick was a train conductor in a past lifetime, and his interest in them has carried over into this lifetime. Personally, I always look for down-to-earth explanations first, but I get excited when there isn't one, and I can entertain possible metaphysical and spiritual explanations.

I remember giving a reading to Michaela, who wanted information on past lifetimes during her session. I saw her living a lifetime a couple hundred years ago as a lighthouse keeper who walked with a limp. He (Michaela) avoided going home to his wife by doing some after-work fishing at a nearby dock. Michaela could relate to this talk of lighthouses. She told me she loves fishing and lighthouses and has an ever-growing collection of miniature lighthouses at home. The second past lifetime I accessed for Michaela included images of her jousting in competitions. I pictured galloping horses, full body armor, fervent crowds chanting for their heroes, sideshow attractions, and food stands. It was a full-blown, medieval state fair in my mind's eye. I could almost smell the funnel cakes and corn dogs! Again, this stirred up familiar, present-day interests for Michaela, and she said in this current lifetime she's always had an unexplained fascination with jousting and renaissance fairs.

Another example is when I gave a reading to Chloe. She wasn't closed off to the idea of past lifetimes. It's just that she had never given it much thought. Since she wasn't raised with conversations of reincarnation, Chloe never developed an opinion on the subject. I started to see visions of her past lifetimes and figured I'd share with her what I was seeing.

I described her recent past lifetime when she was a petite Asian lady whose biggest passion was tending the steep, sloping flower garden that spread up the hill from the back of her house. Chloe was widowed early on in that lifetime, and her love became her flowers, particularly the purple ones. The type of flower didn't necessarily matter, but the purple ones were always her favorite. After I described this, she proceeded to take off her shoe and sock (no, she didn't throw her shoe at me and demand her money back from the reading, if that's what you're thinking). I asked her why she was taking her shoe off.

Chloe smiled at me, and explained that she's always had a strange love for purple flowers. She never knew why until that very moment. There, on the top of her foot, was a big tattoo of a purple hibiscus flower.

While reading another client named Morgan, I concentrated and saw images of her traveling through the jungles of Central America. She was a chaperone, a tour guide for foreigners trekking through the jungle. Leading the way with a rudimentary blade, I saw her hacking through thick brush, escorting her foreign guests. What bothered Morgan more than the heat, the bugs, and the sores on her feet, were the spider webs! Not spiders. Just the massive webs she'd constantly, unintentionally run into face-first. Like feathers sticking to honey, the spider webs itched, tickled, and irritated Morgan's skin on these expeditions until she was on the verge of madness.

After telling this creepy-crawly information to Morgan, her eyes grew wide and she stared at me with a petrified look on her face. "My husband thinks I'm crazy," she said, "but I wake up on a weekly basis in a cold sweat, swatting at my face and wiping off what feels to be spider webs." She explained that she has no fear of spiders in this lifetime, and when she is fully awake, she has no paranoia about them being on her or near her. However, when Morgan dreams at night, she dreams of being in the jungle and having spider webs stuck to her sweaty face.

We just had a breakthrough and possibly arrived at the root of the night terrors. Will Morgan stop having these awful nightmares and stop waking up with the feeling of spider webs on her face? I hope so. Most of the time, bringing a past life issue to the surface is enough to let go of it once and for all. We all can inadvertently access past life memories, both good and bad, in our dreams at night. When we sleep, we access our subconscious, which is the library for all of our past life experiences.

These are just a few accounts I have seen firsthand which lead me to believe that some of our likes and dislikes stem from past life experiences. Fears, phobias, and connections to certain activities from the past can influence us in the present. What do you think? As always, I encourage you to keep an open mind and come to your own conclusions.

Will my loved ones still be in Heaven once I get there, or will they be here living another life already?

Have you ever thrown a party for someone? Maybe a surprise party? You know, where the poor unsuspecting soul celebrating the day of his birth walks into the house and nearly suffers an acute myocardial infarction, scared half to death by the most important people in his life shouting, "SURPRISE!" Nearly scaring someone half to *death* on his *birthday* is ironic to say the least. But more importantly, it's a wondrous occasion and it always makes a person feel special and loved. If you've ever been on the receiving end of a party, then you know the most important aspect is not the funny birthday hats, the music, the table cloths, the decorations, or the cake (okay, *maybe* the cake). The most important aspect of any party is the fact that those you love and care about most are in attendance.

When you die and cross over into Heaven, there's a 99% chance that *everyone* you've loved and lost in this lifetime will be there waiting to greet you. Will they scare the bejesus out of you like it's a surprise party? I'm not sure. I *do* know there will be a welcoming committee, a party for you, and hopefully your favorite cake.

A person usually takes quite a bit of time in Heaven to recover, recuperate, and rejuvenate before coming back to Earth for the next incarnation. Therefore, someone you lost twenty, thirty, or even fifty years ago will most likely still be there by the time you get to Heaven. On very rare occasions, a person may choose to come back to Earth in a relatively quick turnaround, and in that case, may not be present in the welcoming committee when you cross over into Heaven. Again though, this is an exception rather than the norm.

Your loved ones in Heaven miss you just as much as you miss them. They are looking forward to seeing you and catching up. When you cross through the tunnel, over the bridge, or into the light and you step over that threshold into the perfection of Heaven, it will be the most glorious homecoming party you can imagine. And tell those in Heaven to save some cake for the rest of us.

What's the point of living more than once?

Throughout the course of this book, I feel like you and I have gotten to know each other pretty well. I've invested countless hours writing, editing, and sharing myself with you, and you in turn have invested a measurable part of your life reading the content in these pages. I thank you for that, and because of this unspoken bond we've shared, you and I will always be connected. I hope to have altered your life in some positive way. And believe me, simply by picking up this book, you've changed my life for the better.

I must ask you, why did you read this book? For pleasure and leisure? Were you seeking a spiritual awakening? Did you want to expand your horizons and become more open minded? Maybe, you've read this book simply wanting to learn something new. Or to be entertained. Or to laugh. Or to be inspired. Were you seeking growth, intellectually, personally, and spiritually?

Everything I just mentioned are the very same reasons we choose to incarnate time and time again. We incarnate again and again for growth. We do it for inspiration. We do it because we want to learn something new and expand our view on life. The point in living more than one lifetime is the same reason you would read more than one book. Each one is different, and each one has something new to teach.

Andy, do you have any recollection of your past lifetimes?

Throw some popcorn in the microwave, and find a comfy seat. This is a humdinger of a story. You have my word that every component of this story is the truth, the whole truth, and nothing but the truth, so help me God. I also promise you that unlike my good fishing stories, nothing has been exaggerated or embellished here. There are many pieces to this story, so bear with me. To appreciate a good story, you must hear it from the very beginning. So here it is.

I *do* remember one of my past lifetimes. Call it a hunch, an inkling, or a sixth sense, but I have always felt connected to Native American culture. For as long as I can remember, I've had a feeling that one of my most recent past lifetimes took place somewhere in the Midwest. I was a male Native American.

My intuition has always led me to believe that I died in that lifetime from a stomach related ailment. I died alone in a tent or teepee, away from the other members of my tribe. I preferred the solitude. I didn't want pity or attention. I didn't want others to feel uncomfortable, and since there was nothing anyone could do to fix my stomach problem, I wanted to spend my last days in a tent, by myself, preparing to meet my maker. I wasn't lonely. Despite the physical discomfort, I felt complete peace and love, as I took my last breaths. Although I've always known this past life story to be true, I didn't share it with my wife, Kenzie, figuring it was irrelevant.

In my current lifetime, I've always had a feeling that someday, I would have a beautiful little girl who would be highly intuitive. I have always felt she would go on to do great things and would be a wise, kind-hearted, old soul. You should also remember that one of my spirit guides in this current lifetime is named Henry. For as long as I can remember, I've known that Henry was one of my spirit guides. I'm sure that good old Henry was present on the day I met Kenzie for the first time.

Kenzie showed up in my office on a cold day in February. It was 2/3/11 to be exact. This is interesting, considering her favorite numbers are 23 and 11, because her birthday is on 11/23. Upon introducing ourselves to each other, there was a strange familiarity. We felt like old friends. There was a connection that felt as natural as breathing. It seemed as though we were, somehow, in some way, connected. While I was giving Kenzie her reading, a glass candle holder on my shelf exploded into a thousand little pieces, scaring us half to death. I blew out the candle to prevent a fire hazard. In hindsight, it could have been her spirit guides and my spirit guides telling us to pay attention to the significance of our connection.

As I read Kenzie, I established that she had five spirit guides in total, and one of them was named Sarah. Kenzie's face lit up in excitement, and she felt validated. She then told me she's always had a feeling Sarah was the name of her main spirit guide, and she's always felt she had five spirit guides in total.

We continued talking, and Kenzie told me that she is one-fourth Native American. Her biological father is one-half Sioux. After hearing her say this, I noticed subtle Native American features in her eyes and cheekbones. She was beautiful for sure. Not only by outward appearance, but the beauty of her spirit was easy to see as well. I explained to her that I could see her having a little girl someday who would end up being a compassionate and intuitive person who would go on to make huge, positive changes in the world. As Kenzie's reading came to an end, we parted ways with a handshake, despite the fact that we both secretly felt compelled to hug.

Some time went by. Kenzie and I stayed in touch through a metaphysical discussion group I facilitate once a month. When the time was right, we let our guards down and began to fall for each other. It didn't take long for us to say, "I love you." We would daydream about our future together and talk about possible baby names for our future children.

We put more emphasis on thinking of *girl* baby names, since I have always known I would have a girl, and in the reading I gave Kenzie, I said she would have a special little girl as well. I came up with a beautiful and unique name, and I convinced Kenzie it would be just perfect for our future daughter. Our daughter's name would be Sky. Someday, when the time was right, we would bring this precious, beautiful old soul into the world.

A little more time went by, and I was scheduled to give lectures at a metaphysical fair. As I was giving my lectures, Kenzie sought out a reputable hypnotist who was offering past life regressions at the event. As Kenzie was put into a meditative state, the hypnotist asked her what images she could see. Kenzie reported being in a Native American community in the Midwest of the United States. When asked who her best friend was, she replied, "My husband, Andy, is my best friend." Although my name most likely would not have been Andy in the past lifetime, the hypnotist assumed this meant I was present in that life and was her husband.

When the hypnotist asked who else was present in that lifetime, Kenzie replied, "Our best friends, Henry and Sarah Cloud." The hypnotherapist then asked Kenzie, "And what is *your* name in this lifetime?" Kenzie replied, "Miah. Maya. Something like that. I can't really pronounce it." During this regression, Kenzie also mentioned that her husband (me) died in a tent, all alone, after taking an accidental arrow through the stomach.

After her regression was over and we left the metaphysical fair, Kenzie excitedly shared with me the information from her past life regression. I got goose bumps hearing the part about the arrow in my stomach and how she reported I died in a tent all by myself. After all, I *never* shared that information with her before. What also seemed interesting about the regression was the fact that Kenzie mentioned Henry and Sarah (who are our current spirit guides).

Later that night, Kenzie attempted to find an old, handwritten family tree that was passed down to her many years ago. She kept it in an old shoebox and hadn't looked at it for several years. Kenzie could not remember the names of those in her family tree and wanted to refresh her memory. After fishing it out and scrolling through all the names in the family tree, Kenzie nearly fainted in disbelief. It showed that in the 1800s, there was a married Native American couple in her family named Sarah and Henry Cloud. With butterflies in her stomach and her hair standing on end, Kenzie was speechless as she stared at the old family tree.

So there it was. My spirit guide Henry and her spirit guide Sarah were real people who had lived before. They were husband and wife who lived in the 1800s as members of the Sioux Tribe. Henry and Sarah were our best friends in the past lifetime, and since then, they have become spirit guides for Kenzie and me. Not many people can claim to have their spirit guide in their family trees, but Kenzie can. The story is almost over, but there's one more interesting twist.

If you remember correctly, months prior to Kenzie's past life regression, I came up with the name Sky for our future daughter. We would talk about her often and looked forward to someday welcoming her into this world. In Kenzie's regression, the hypnotherapist asked what name Kenzie went by in that past lifetime, and although she couldn't quite pronounce it, she said something to the effect of "Miah or Maya." Later that night, after finding her family tree in the old shoebox, Kenzie decided to look up some Native American words from the Sioux language, attempting to piece together any missing aspects to this story.

While conducting this research, she came across a name that brought tears to her eyes. Mahpiya. It means "sky" or "heavenly" in the Sioux language, and it's the closest word she could find to Miah or Maya. Mahpiya was Kenzie's name in the past lifetime we shared together. Kenzie's name was Sky.

It's funny how you can miss someone you've technically never met before. Someday, we will hold our precious baby girl. We will call her Sky. We'll look into her soulful eyes, and wonder how many times she's been here on Earth before. We'll tell her she's destined for big things that will make this world a better place. Someday, we'll tell her a story about a married couple named Henry and Sarah who lived a long time ago, and how they still help mommy and daddy in spirit form. We'll tell Sky about a glass candle holder that exploded during a very special psychic reading many years ago on a cold, February day. We'll tell her a love story, a real life fairy tale of how her parents' connection goes beyond this lifetime. And we'll explain how, in a cosmic turn of events, she is named after her mother, who was also named Sky in a past lifetime.

After submitting this book to WriteLife Publishing, Andy and Kenzie learned they were pregnant with their first child. It's a girl.

Conclusion

Sitting here in my office, I'm looking out the window and pondering how to conclude this book. Brisk fall days such as these always leave me feeling sentimental and philosophical. As I look out at the blazing orange and yellow leaves of the trees, I feel saddened that we've come to the end of our journey together. Much like the leaves will soon part ways with their branches, I too must say goodbye for now. Rest assured, you and I will cross paths again in the future. We'll pick up right where we left off, just like good friends always do. And we'll take more adventures together, discussing angels, ghosts, marvelous mysteries, and psychic synchronicity. This is just the beginning.

So how do we conclude a wild journey that's zipped us back and forth across the emotional spectrum? Your guess is as good as mine. Maybe, we shouldn't *conclude* anything. Perhaps we should not end this book with a period. Let's part ways with an, "Until next time..." A "See ya later," will do.

Until we meet again in the pages of my next book, please keep some things in mind. Next time you go to a circus, buy a pirate sword. When you watch your child color on the driveway with sidewalk chalk, know that your loved ones in Heaven are looking down, reading the message. When you feel a comforting wave of déjà vu wash over you, remember it's your soul's recollection of a wonderful and crazy life you planned for yourself long before you ever arrived here.

You are psychic. That intuitive compass God placed in your pocket will help you find your true north. Believe that angels are real. They come in all shapes and sizes. Some with wings, some with brown fur, and others warm our hands on cold winter nights. Take comfort in knowing that somewhere out there is a spirit guide named "Lefty" who played baseball here on Earth once upon a time. Remember that your very own spirit guides have "got you covered," no matter what. And if a flying paint roller from Heaven is headed your way, don't run. Smile, and know that it's coming from a good place. A place you've often called Home.

About the Author

Andy Myers is a full-time psychic medium, life coach, and inspirational speaker. He is breaking the psychic stereotype with his genuine and down-to-earth approach to intuition. Andy is nationally known for his work, and people wait nearly an entire year to have a session with him. His accurate, validating, and compassionate readings have changed the lives of thousands. He travels often to conduct psychic events in major cities around the country. Andy has been featured on radio stations nationwide, and is the annual keynote speaker at the Omaha Health Expo. He has a Bachelor's Degree in Social Work from the University of Nebraska at Omaha. Andy is happily married and lives in Omaha.

www.andymyersonline.com